EXECUTIVE EDITOR
Natalie Earnheart

CREATIVE TEAM
Jenny Doan, Natalie Earnheart, Christine Ricks,
Tyler MacBeth, Mike Brunner, Lauren Dorton,
Jennifer Dowling, Dustin Weant, Jessica Toye,
Kimberly Forman, Denise Lane

EDITORS & COPYWRITERS
Nichole Spravzoff, Camille Maddox,
David Litherland, Julie Barber-Arutyunyan

SEWIST TEAM
Jenny Doan, Natalie Earnheart, Courtenay Hughes,
Carol Henderson, Janice Richardson,
Aislinn Earnheart, Janet Yamamoto

PRINTING COORDINATOR
Rob Stoebener

PRINTING SERVICES
Walsworth Print Group
803 South Missouri
Marceline, MO 64658

LOCATIONS
Duncan Berry Farm, Smithville, MO
Tim and Liz Leader, Hamilton, MO
Susie Pipkin, Hamilton, MO
Jennifer Dowling, Hamilton, MO

CONTACT US
Missouri Star Quilt Company
114 N Davis
Hamilton, MO 64644
888-571-1122
info@missouriquiltco.com

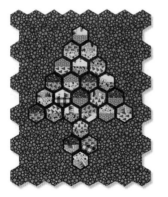

contents

Oops! Sometimes we make mistakes. To find corrections to every issue of BLOCK go to: **www.msqc.co/corrections**

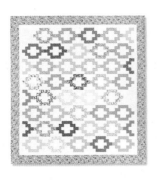

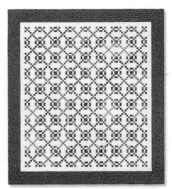

A note from Jenny

Savor the Simple Moments

Dear Quilters,

This year has been so completely out of the ordinary and challenging in so many ways that I find myself simplifying again and experiencing great joy in the things that I have often taken for granted. Now, preparing for the holiday season is less about the hustle and bustle of finding just the right present, but taking the time to help create a warm, welcoming spirit in my home and in my community.

As I contemplate the spirit of generosity, I recognize that giving comes in many forms. Some give of their time and energy, some share love abundantly and easily, some can listen for hours, some give the biggest hugs, and some create handmade gifts to share. There are many ways to be generous and no matter how you like to give, your intentions absolutely matter. As we've experienced, the simplest gift from a child—a crumpled flower, a scribbled picture, or a sloppy kiss—can mean so much. Their intention comes through, as does ours. Never give in to the thought that your offering is insufficient. If you've given from the heart, that's all that truly matters.

Considering the state of our nation, we could all use an extra boost of kindness. Let's make this season a time to truly give from the heart and reach out to our loved ones. Let's slow down, savor the simple moments with friends and family, and do the things that bring us joy. Please remember, you're always welcome at Missouri Star and you are all family to me.

JENNY DOAN
MISSOURI STAR QUILT CO.

4

GET YOUR **DIGITAL ISSUE** TODAY!

Did you know that with every issue of BLOCK, you also get a FREE digital copy online? Access it in your Missouri Star account **RIGHT NOW!**

Sue Daley: Queen of English Paper Piecing

"As much as I love using the sewing machine, I soon realized that I loved hand sewing more."

Say hello to Sue Daley, a lovely Australian quilter with a passion for English paper piecing. She lives on the beautiful Sunshine Coast. Typically, her days are filled with designing and teaching across Australia and all over the world, but lately she's been spending some quality time at home, as we all have been. We took a moment to catch up with her and learn more about who she is and why she's been called the "Queen of English paper piecing."

Can you tell us about yourself and how you got into sewing and quilting?
"I started sewing much like many other people. I started making my own clothes at school when I was just 9 years old. There were no sewing machines so it was all done by hand using French seams. However, at home my mother taught me to use her sewing machine, which you can imagine was so much quicker. My passion for patchwork began in 1980, when I was expecting my first child. I made one quilt a year for three years. After my third child was born I decided I could get a little more serious now that I had a little girl. Obsessive is probably the best way to describe it now, with most of my days being filled with designing, teaching, and mentoring across Australia and all over the world."

Shown on Left Page:
Quatro Colour by Sue Daley

What was your first quilt or sewing project? What have you learned since then?

"My first quilt was terrible, made while I was pregnant with my first son. I used red and white polyester fabric using 6" squares which I cut out with scissors and using ½" seam allowance to sew it up. At that time, we didn't have the luxury of rotary cutters and cutting mats, etc. here in Australia. (All the important things in life, right?) Boy, have I learnt a lot since then. Most importantly I mastered the art of the ¼" seam allowance using my sewing machine. As much as I love using the sewing machine, I soon realized that I loved hand sewing more."

What inspires you to create your beautiful English paper piecing designs?

"Inspiration comes from anywhere and everywhere you just have to be open to it. I love color and how it all plays together to create so many beautiful and amazing things. However, when I first started English paper piecing I just wanted to simplify the technique so it was more user friendly for people to do as it was so time consuming."

"English paper piecing is an age old art and although I didn't invent this technique, I sure hope that I have made it much easier. My paper and template business was the first in Australia and is now servicing the entire world. I then introduced the Glue Pen method to the industry and this notion single-handedly changed the entire technique. I feel that I have been able to turn a world of machine piecers around and show them that it's not just about the sewing machine, we can, in fact, enjoy both techniques together."

Why do you sew? How does it help you express your creativity?

"I sew simply because I love it. Putting colors together, fussy cutting fabrics to make new designs is so much fun. Often, I start down one path only to find myself heading down a different one and that's exciting to me. I believe slow stitching is good for the soul in this crazy busy world we live in."

> "English paper piecing is an age old art and although I didn't invent this technique, I sure hope that I have made it much easier."

Is there anything else you'd like to add?

"In all of the years I have been creating and sewing, it is only over the last couple of years and more so in the past six months that I have realized it is so much more than just creating and sewing. It is a way that people can come together to share a passion, to be inspired, to laugh together, and to cry together. I consider myself very privileged to have been on this amazing creative journey. To have traveled the world teaching, talking, and inspiring others with something that I am so passionate about. I will be forever grateful to everyone that has supported me over the years."

Windchime by Sue Daley

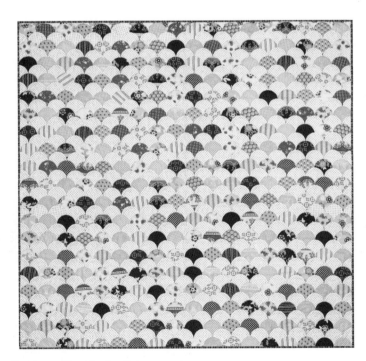

Raspberry Clams by Sue Daley

How to Get Started:

English paper piecing may seem like a complex technique to master, but with the right tools, and a little know-how, it becomes incredibly doable! First of all, it doesn't require a sewing machine—all you need is a needle, thread, template, and fabric to get started. It's the perfect project to tote along if you're a quilter on the go, and it's an excellent way to occupy time while waiting or traveling. English paper piecing fits easily in a bag or a purse to accompany you wherever you go. Work on a small section at a time, sew them all together, and suddenly, you have a big, beautiful masterpiece!

9

Just a few years ago, we welcomed Sue Daley to Missouri Star for her incredible English paper piecing retreat and we've loved EPP ever since! Her workshop was a patchwork paradise. Sue became fast friends with Jenny and together they continue to teach the beauty of EPP to quilters around the world.

Up and Away Pincushion

by Sue Daley

materials

PROJECT SIZE
Approximately 2½" diameter

PROJECT SUPPLIES
Small pieces of fabric in
  3 contrasting colors
Fiber or pincushion fill
(12) 1½" Pentagon* precut papers

This pincushion can be made with any size pentagon papers.

1 instructions

Following the English paper piecing instructions, make the pincushion top and bottom as shown in the diagrams, joining the sides as indicated by the arrows. **1A 1B**

Join the 2 sections together leaving 2 edges open at the bottom to allow for turning out and stuffing.

Remove papers and turn right sides out. Fill firmly with fiber or pincushion fill. Sew the opening closed.

Optional: Glue a large button on the base to help the cushion stand upright and add a decorative whipped running stitch around the seams as shown in the photo.

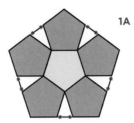

1A

pincushion top

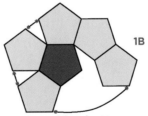

1B

pincushion bottom

2 english paper piecing general requirement

- Sue Daley Designs Size 11 or Size 15 Milliners needles — The finer the needles the neater your stitches will be.

- Sue Daley Sewline Glue Pen.

- Wonderfil Deco Bob thread for sewing the pieces together. When you sew the pieces together the thread drags across the top of the card and it shreds therefore weakening the thread. Wonderfil Deco Bob is a polyester thread and is extremely strong. The thread is very fine and it is not necessary to have lots of colors as it blends well and disappears into the fabric.

3 the Sue Daley glue pen method

These instructions apply to all shapes when paper piecing.

Fold your fabric into layers if necessary and place your acrylic template on top of the fabric and rotary cut around the shape (you can cut up to 6 pieces at a time).

Hint: If you are fussy cutting you will need to cut 1 shape out at a time on the same pattern repeat of the fabric for as many shapes as you need.

Lay your fabric shape wrong side up and place the paper shape on top making sure you center it. **3A 3B**

Run the glue pen along 1 side of the paper shape, keeping the glue away from the edge of the paper. Be careful not to take it over the edge onto the fabric (this will cause a build-up making it difficult to stitch through). **3C 3D**

Fold the fabric over and hold for a moment. Continue around the shape in the 1 direction until all sides are turned over. **3E 3F 3G**

11

Note:

1. Don't use too much glue. You will get the hang of it after you have done a few.

2. In the warm weather the glue can become soft (i.e. you will use too much). I suggest putting it in the fridge for a few minutes.

3. If you use too much glue and the papers are hard to remove, press with a steam iron and it will relax the glue allowing you to remove the papers more easily.

Note: With some of the shapes the corners will fold in nice and neatly (e.g. the hexagon) and others (e.g. diamonds or pies) don't. See the diagram **3G**. Leave the tails hanging out making sure that the fabric is nice and tight around the card.

4 assemble the pieces

Place right sides together and make a knicker knot.

The Knicker Knot

Pass the needle through all layers to start the knot. **4A**

Take the single thread and pass under the needle to the left. **4B**

Take the double thread and do the opposite — pass to the right side of the needle. Wrapping underneath and around the needle. **4C**

Pull the thread through to create the knot. **4D**

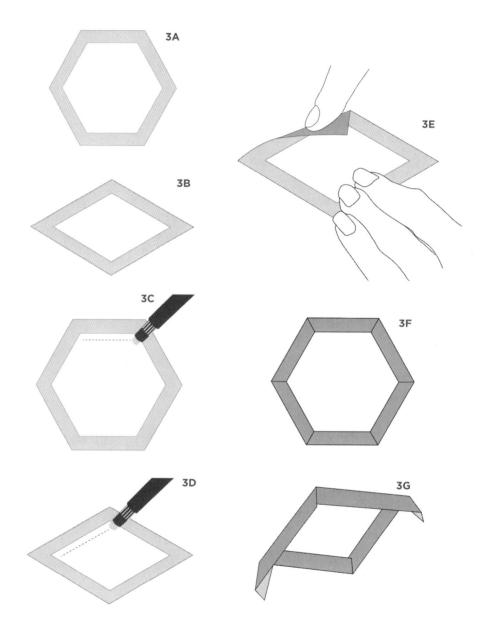

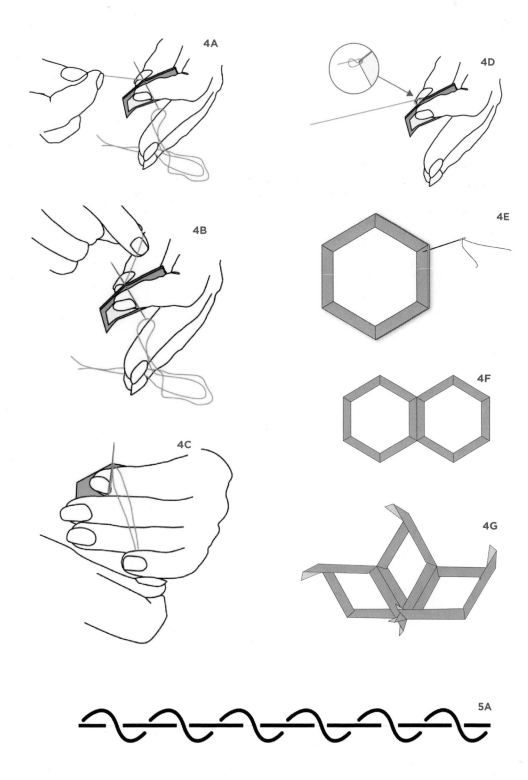

4A

4B

4C

4D

4E

4F

4G

Whip stitch from corner to corner. **4E**

Note: Always start with a knicker knot and finish with a knicker knot.

Open them out and with a dry iron give them a press. **4F 4G**

Note:

1. When sewing stars or pies together do not sew the tails in. They will automatically lay flat behind your work.

2. When sewing stars or pies make sure that you sew 2 halves and then sew them together with 1 seam through the middle. This will eliminate having a hole in the center of your work.

Paper can be removed once the blocks are surrounded and stabilized by other blocks. Gently peel the fabric back from the papers.

Note: If you are having problems peeling the fabric back from the paper, you have probably used too much glue. Just dampen slightly with water which will soften the glue and help you to peel back the fabric.

Papers can be reused a number of times.

5 whipped running stitch

Running: 2 strands
Whipping: 6 strands

Hint: Be careful not to pull your thread too tight. **5A**

5A

13

For the tutorial and everything
you need to make this project visit:
www.msqc.co/Blockv7issue4

Homespun Holiday Traditions
Pop Stars Quilt

We humans have found so many interesting ways to celebrate the important moments of our lives. To some, these traditions can seem weird or strange; for example, one of the core parts of a traditional German wedding is getting the bride and groom together after the vows, handing them a log and a lumberjack-sized saw, and having them saw it in half! It seems a bit goofy at face value, but if you ask about it, Germans describe it as the first obstacle a newlywed couple has to face together with teamwork and communication. So beyond the face value, it's actually very meaningful and sweet!

A family friend told me about a holiday tradition that she had thought was strange: When she was young, her great aunt had a large cabin out in the country, so she would always host the family get-togethers around the holidays. One of her earliest memories was going out to the cabin for Thanksgiving, only to find all of the rafters covered in quilts! They were hung all across the house, in nearly every room, and sometimes it would be hard to go through a room without moving one aside. It made for great hide-and-seek for the kids, but my friend always found it just a bit strange growing up.

Many years went by like this, and each year the quilts were hung up. Each quilt was unique, with different designs, colors, and sizes. Sometimes the king sized quilts would be hung up like dividers in the bedrooms, and others would be draped over the rafters above the dining room while they ate. My friend could never figure out any rhyme or reason to where each quilt was hung up, but never thought to ask about it.

As it usually happens, the great aunt unfortunately passed away several years ago. My friend, now with a family of her own and a bevy of quilts, attended her funeral, only to find the church where it was held covered in quilts as well! Draped over every pew, hanging from the wall, and laid out on the floor, the quilts completely covered the church. After the service, my friend finally asked about the quilts; where had the great aunt gotten them, and why did she display them in such an eccentric way?

It turns out that the great aunt had been collecting the quilts from all across the family for decades. She had dozens of quilts, some nearly a century old! She hung them up each year in order to treasure the history that each quilt held, and to continue their stories with the next generations. My friend was so touched by this, that she took up her great aunt's stewardship for herself! While her collection is not quite as big, each year, little by little, it grows and is hung up for all to see around the holidays.

What unique traditions does your family follow? Write to us at blockstories@missouriquiltco.com and share your little holiday eccentricities so that we can all learn a little something to treasure (and maybe adopt for ourselves).

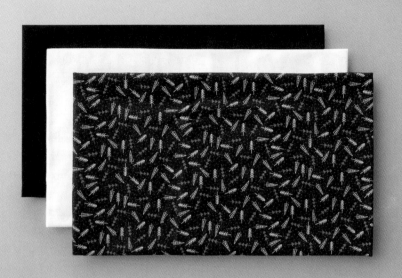

materials

QUILT SIZE
67" x 75½"

BLOCK SIZE
9" unfinished, 8½" finished

QUILT TOP
1 package 10" print squares
½ yard accent fabric
1¾ yards background fabric
  - includes inner border

OUTER BORDER
1¼ yards

BINDING
¾ yard

BACKING
4¾ yards - vertical seam(s)
  or 2½ yards of 108" wide

SAMPLE QUILT
The Christmas Card by Sweetwater
for Moda Fabrics

1A

2A

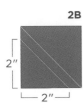

2B

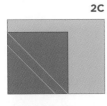

2C

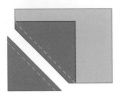

1 cut

Sort the 10″ print squares into 8 dark print squares and 34 light print squares.

Note: If the number of dark and light prints in your package of 10″ squares is different, you can adjust your blocks and layout. You will need to alter the number of background and accent squares cut later in this section—(8) 2½″ background squares are needed for each light print set and (8) 2½″ accent squares are needed for each dark print set.

Stack as many of your selected squares as you feel comfortable cutting at 1 time on your cutting surface. Cut (2) 3″ strips from 1 side of the stacked squares, being careful not to disturb the fabric, then cut (2) 3″ widths across the strips from your squares. You will have (4) 3″ squares, (4) 3″ x 4″ rectangles and (1) 4″ square from each of your 10″ print squares. Keep all matching squares and rectangles together in sets. Cut **42 sets**. **1A**

From the accent fabric, cut (4) 2½″ strips across the width of the fabric. Cut (16) 2½″ squares from each strip for a **total of 64** accent squares.

From the background fabric, cut (17) 2½″ strips across the width of the fabric. Cut (16) 2½″ squares from each strip for a **total of 272** background squares. Set the remaining background fabric aside for the inner and pieced borders.

2 snowball corners

Mark a diagonal line corner to corner on each background and accent square with a fabric pen or pencil. **2A**

Select a background square and measure up from 1 corner of the square, make a mark at 2″. Measure 2″ from the same corner across the bottom of the square and mark. Draw a line between the 2 marks parallel to your first diagonal line. Repeat drawing the second diagonal line on a **total of 144** background squares. **2B**

To snowball the corners for your light print sets, layer a background square with 2 marked lines atop a 3″ x 4″ light print rectangle with right sides together as shown. Sew on both diagonal lines. Cut between the 2 sewn lines. **2C**

Open and press each piece toward the background fabric. Set the half-square triangle aside for the pieced border. **2D**

Repeat to snowball the opposite corner as shown and make a second half-square triangle. **2E**

Continue to snowball 2 corners of each 3″ x 4″ light print rectangle, keeping the snowballed units, 3″ squares, and 4″ squares of matching light prints together in sets. Once all of the 144 double-marked background squares have been used, continue with the squares that have 1 diagonal line. Keep the sets of snowballed units, 3″ squares, and 4″ squares of matching light prints together.

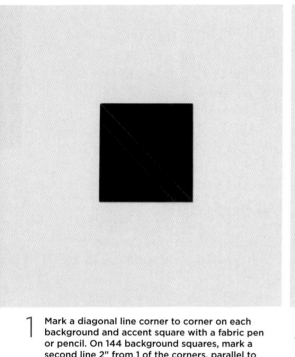

1   Mark a diagonal line corner to corner on each background and accent square with a fabric pen or pencil. On 144 background squares, mark a second line 2″ from 1 of the corners, parallel to the first line.

2   Lay a background square with 2 marked lines atop a 3″ x 4″ light print rectangle with right sides together as shown. Sew on both diagonal lines. Cut between the 2 sewn lines.

3   Open and press each piece toward the background fabric. Set the half-square triangle aside for the pieced border.

4   Repeat to snowball the opposite corner as shown and make a second half-square triangle.

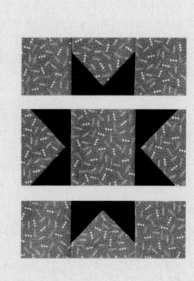

5   Select a matching set. Sew a 3″ square to each side of a snowballed unit. Make 2 outer rows. Sew a snowballed unit to each side of a 4″ square as shown to make the center row. Arrange the 2 outer rows and 1 center row as shown.

6   Nest the seams and sew the rows together to complete the block. Make 42 blocks.

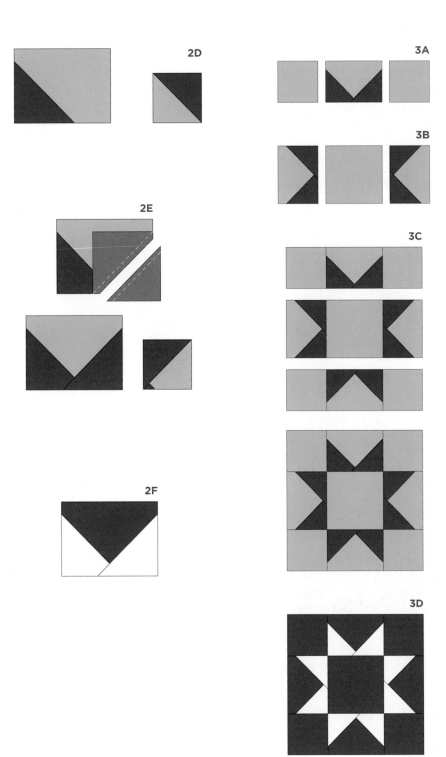

2D

2E

2F

3A

3B

3C

3D

Repeat the previous instructions to snowball 2½" accent squares to 2 corners of each 3" x 4" dark print rectangle, keeping the sets of snowballed units, 3" squares, and 4" squares of matching dark prints together. **2F**

3 block construction

Select a matching set. Sew a 3" square to each side of a snowballed unit. Press the seams toward the squares. **Make 2** outer rows. **3A**

Sew a snowballed unit to each side of a 4" square, noting the orientation in the diagram. Press the seams toward the square. **Make 1** center row. **3B**

Arrange the 2 outer rows and 1 center row as shown. Nest the seams and sew the rows together to complete the block. **Make 42** blocks. **3C 3D**

Block Size: 9" unfinished, 8½" finished

4 arrange & sew

Referring to the diagram on page 21, lay out your blocks in **7 rows** of **6 blocks** each. Sew the blocks together in rows. Press the seam allowances of all odd-numbered rows to the left and all even-numbered rows to the right. Nest the seams and sew the rows together to complete the quilt center.

5 inner border

Cut (6) 1½" strips across the width of the background fabric. Sew the strips together end-to-end to make 1 long strip. Trim the borders from this strip. Set the remaining background fabric aside for the pieced border.

Refer to Borders (pg. 110) in the Construction Basics to measure, cut, and attach the inner borders. The strips are approximately 60" for the sides and approximately 53½" for the top and bottom.

6 pieced border

From the background fabric, cut (1) 2" strip across the width of the fabric. Subcut (4) 2" squares and set them aside for the moment. Set the remaining piece of strip aside for another project.

Square each of the half-square triangles set aside earlier to 2" if needed.

Sew 2 matching half-square triangles together as shown. **Make 72** pieced units. **6A**

Refer to Borders (pg. 110) in the Construction Basics to measure the length of your quilt top at this point. The pieced borders will be made to match these measurements and are approximately 62" for the sides.

Using a scant ¼" seam, sew 19 pieced units side by side to create a pieced side border. Adjustments can be made by taking in or letting out seams as needed to match the length of your quilt center. **Make 2**. **6B**

Refer to the diagram on page 21 as needed and sew a pieced border to each side of the quilt top.

Refer to Borders (pg. 110) of the Construction Basics to measure the width of your quilt top. The pieced borders will be made to match these measurements and are approximately 56½" for the top and bottom.

6A

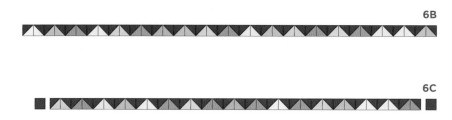

6B

6C

Using a scant ¼" seam, sew 17 pieced units side by side to create a pieced border. Sew a 2" background square to each end of the pieced strip. **Make 2** pieced borders for the top and bottom. Again, adjustments can be made by taking in or letting out seams as needed to match the width of your quilt top. **6C**

Refer to the diagram to the left as needed and sew a pieced border to the top and bottom of the quilt top.

7 outer border

Cut (7) 6" strips across the width of the outer border fabric. Sew the strips together end-to-end to make 1 long strip. Trim the borders from this strip.

Refer to Borders (pg. 110) in the Construction Basics to measure, cut, and attach the outer borders. The strips are approximately 65" for the sides and approximately 67½" for the top and bottom.

8 quilt & bind

Layer the quilt with batting and backing and quilt. After the quilting is complete, square up the quilt and trim away all excess batting and backing. Add binding to complete the quilt. See Construction Basics (pg. 110) for binding instructions.

For the tutorial and everything you need to make this quilt visit: www.msqc.co/Blockv7issue4

Catching the Quilting Bug

Every Which Way But Goose Quilt

My young friends Emily and Kyle started dating just as summertime was ending. The gentle autumn weather beckoned to those two love birds, and for weeks on end they soaked up every moment they could outside. And everywhere they went, Kyle's quilt went, too.

It was an old blue and white flower basket made from cheater cloth by his sweet grandmother. She had tied the quilt with blue yarn and finished it off with a prairie point binding. Over the years, the fabric had been worn to a perfect softness. It was the kind of quilt you could take along anywhere and not worry about dirt or spills. It was an adventure quilt.

That quilt had been a permanent fixture in the back of Kyle's rusty Jeep since high school, and it sort of became a symbol of his courtship with Emily. All through September and October, they took the quilt on picnics and to the drive-in movie. Emily wrapped it around her shoulders during Kyle's adult league softball games. It kept them warm on the Halloween hayride through the park and the last fishing trip of the season. And that's when the adventure quilt was lost.

It had been a glorious day of fishing at a mountain lake surrounded by golden-leaved aspens. They stayed late enough to watch the sun set over the water. Just as stars started to peek through the branches of towering lodgepole pines, Kyle and Emily packed up and hit the road.

But as they wound their way through the dark, an enormous black figure emerged from the forest and planted itself directly in their path. "Moose!" shrieked Emily as Kyle brought his Jeep to a screeching halt. He cranked the wheel to avoid the hulking figure, and

in the process, hit a small boulder on the side of the road. The front passenger tire exploded.

So by the light of a half moon, Kyle pulled the spare tire off the back of the Jeep. Emily grabbed the quilt and set it on a fallen log so she could reach the jack. In just a few minutes, the tire was changed and they were back on the road. Unfortunately, the adventure quilt was still on that log, and no one noticed for days.

Emily felt terrible for losing the quilt. She decided she was going to make a replacement adventure quilt as a birthday surprise for Kyle.

Though she came from a long line of talented quilters, Emily had not sewn a stitch since seventh grade sewing class. She couldn't even thread a machine! But with the help of her mother, she gathered the courage to try a simple charm quilt.

Every night before bed, Emily sewed one long row of charms. It was a nice way to end the day, but nothing earth-shattering. But, when she started to join those rows together, something ignited in her soul and she simply could not stop! Emily sewed into the wee hours of the morning and those strips were quickly transformed into a full size quilt top.

You can probably guess that the new adventure quilt was only the first of many. Emily had caught the quilting bug that we all know so well. But even after conquering Dresdens, Y-seams, and appliqué, the adventure quilt was always her favorite. Eventually, the rusty old Jeep was replaced with a minivan full of booster seats and crumbs, and everywhere they went, that adventure quilt went, too, gathering little rips, stains, and memories all along the way!

materials

QUILT SIZE
76″ x 84″

BLOCK SIZE
8½″ x 16½″ unfinished,
8″ x 16″ finished

QUILT TOP
4 packages 5″ print squares
4 packages 5″ background squares
½ yard coordinating print fabric
1 yard background fabric
  - includes border

BINDING
¾ yard

BACKING
5¼ yards – vertical seam(s)
  or 2½ yards 108″ wide

SAMPLE QUILT
Wilmington Essentials - Bubble Up
by Hello Angel for Wilmington Prints

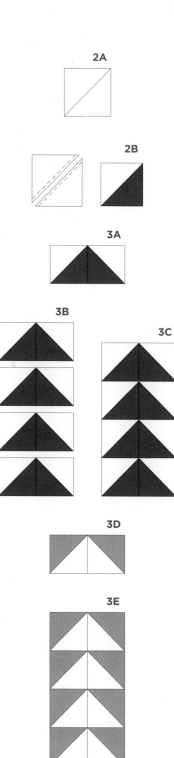

2A

2B

3A

3B

3C

3D

3E

1 sort & cut

From the coordinating print fabric, cut (2) 5″ strips across the width of the fabric. Subcut 5″ squares from the strips. Each strip will yield 8 squares and a **total of 12** are needed. Add these squares to your packages of 5″ print squares. Set the remainder of the fabric aside for another project.

Sort the 5″ print squares into a **total of 45** sets of 4 matching squares.

From the background fabric, cut (2) 5″ strips across the width of the fabric. Subcut into 5″ squares. Each strip will yield 8 squares and you will need to add 12 squares to your packages for a **total of 180** background squares. Set the remaining background fabric aside for the border.

2 make half-square triangles

Mark a line from corner to corner once on the diagonal on the reverse side of each background square. **2A**

Choose 1 set of print squares. Place a marked background square atop a print square with right sides facing. Sew on both sides of the marked line using a ¼″ seam allowance. Cut on the marked line. Open each unit and press the seams toward the darker fabric. Trim the units

to 4½″ square. Each pair of sewn squares will yield 2 half-square triangles. Repeat with the remaining print squares in your selected set to **make 8** matching half-square triangles. Keep the set of matching units together. **2B**

Repeat to make a **total of 45** sets of 8 matching half-square triangles with all of the remaining squares.

3 block construction

Select 1 set of matching half-square triangles. Sew 2 half-square triangles together as shown with the print sides together. **Make 4** flying geese units. **3A**

Press the seams of 2 flying geese units to the right and the seams of the other 2 units to the left. Arrange the 4 units as shown with the seams alternating left and right. Nest the seams and sew the 4 units together. Press the seams toward the bottom. **Make 23** A blocks. **3B 3C**

Select another set of matching half-square triangles. Sew 2 half-square triangles together as shown, this time with the background sides together. **Make 4** flying geese units. **3D**

In the same manner as before, press and sew the 4 units together. Press the seams toward the bottom. **Make 22** B blocks. **3E**

Block Size: 8½″ x 16½″ unfinished, 8″ x 16″ finished

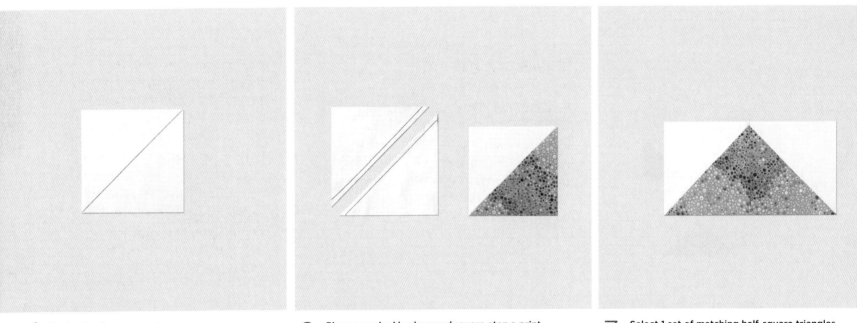

1 Mark a line from corner to corner once on the diagonal on the reverse side of each background square.

2 Place a marked background square atop a print square, right sides facing. Sew on both sides of the marked line using a ¼" seam allowance. Cut on the marked line and press. Trim to 4½". Repeat to make a total of 45 sets of 8 matching half-square triangles with all of the remaining squares.

3 Select 1 set of matching half-square triangles. Sew 2 half-square triangles together as shown, print sides together. Make 4 flying geese units.

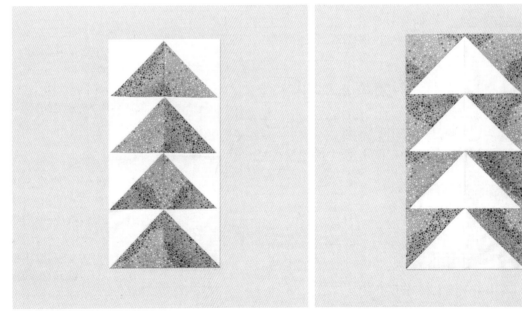

4 Arrange the 4 units as shown with the seams alternating left and right. Nest the seams and sew the 4 units together. Press the seams toward the bottom. Make 23 A blocks.

5 Sew 2 half-square triangles together as shown, this time with the background sides together. Make 4 flying geese units. In the same manner as before, sew the 4 units together. Make 22 B blocks.

4 arrange & sew

Referring to the diagram below, lay out your blocks in **5 rows** of **9 blocks** each.

Each odd-numbered row will begin with an A block and alternate with B blocks which are turned 180° so the arrows point down.

Each even-numbered row will begin with a B block and alternate with A blocks which are turned 180° so the arrows point down.

Sew the blocks together in rows. Press the seams of the odd-numbered rows to the left and the seams of the even-numbered rows to the right. Nest the seams and sew the rows together to complete the quilt center. Press the seams toward the bottom.

5 border

Cut (8) 2½" strips across the width of the background fabric. Sew the strips together end-to-end to make 1 long strip. Trim the border from this strip.

Refer to Borders (pg. 110) in the Construction Basics to measure, cut, and attach the borders. The strips are approximately 80½" for the sides and approximately 76½" for the top and bottom.

6 quilt & bind

Layer the quilt with batting and backing and quilt. After the quilting is complete, square up the quilt and trim away all excess batting and backing. Add binding to complete the quilt. See Construction Basics (pg. 110) for binding instructions.

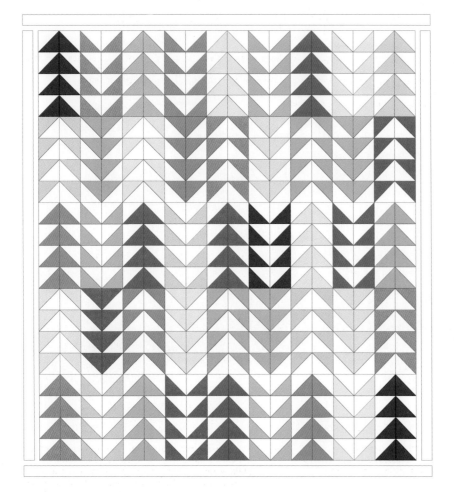

For the tutorial and everything
you need to make this quilt visit:
www.msqc.co/Blockv7issue4

Planning Ahead for the Holidays
Quilt As You Go Holiday Hexies Advent Calendar

Let's be realistic, here. Not all of us have time to create thoughtful presents months in advance for the holidays, not even me. Even if our intentions are there, the time may be short, and I completely understand that. I have some easy solutions to help you create wonderful homemade gifts, even if you're short on time. Treat yourself kindly and be realistic about your capacity to create handmade presents, that way you'll actually be able to enjoy your holiday preparations!

Count Down to Christmas
An advent calender is a thoughtful gift that gets used every year! Try a fun quilt as you go Hexagon pattern in festive colors for the gift that keeps on giving.

Hung by the Chimney with Care
Homemade stockings are a lovely gift to give, and they can be used year after year as well. Fill them up with their favorite treats, attach a nametag to them, and you're good to go!

Gnome, Sweet Gnome
If a full size quilt is out of the question, why not a pretty wall hanging or a table topper? They come together in a snap! Missouri Star's Winter Wall Hanging featuring cute gnomes is one of my favorites.

Serve Up Some Cheer
Aprons and matching hot pads are a thoughtful gift for the baker in the family. And for hot pads, pick up special insulated batting to keep their hands from getting too toasty.

Roll Out the Rug
Have you seen those amazing jelly roll rugs? They are so neat and all you need is your favorite roll of 2½" strips and a bundle of Katahdin batting strips.

Tote-ally Amazing
A handmade tote bag or purse would be greatly appreciated by fashionable friends and family. Choose fabric in their favorite colors and stitch up a beautiful, useful gift they'll love.

Merry and Bright
A set of matching fabric storage boxes or even those amazing rope bowls might be just the thing. They add a handmade touch to their home decor while keeping everything organized.

Everyone's Welcome at the Table
Place mats come together quickly as well and make the table setting look so nice. Create a matching set for the entire family and add embroidered names for a personalized touch.

Something for the Kids
Set aside the endless piecing and pick your favorite quilt panel to make fast, fun quilts for the little ones. They also make cute baby books, darling wall hangings, and stuffed animals.

Add Some Sparkle
For those who enjoy sewing, we all know that you can never have enough pincushions. Whip together a sweet little pincushion for them and add a shiny new set of pins.

Top the Tree
In some families, there's a tradition of giving each other Christmas tree ornaments every year. Why not create personalized handmade ornaments for everyone?

Check out the digital issue of BLOCK free with your subscription for even more holiday gift ideas and easy tutorials!

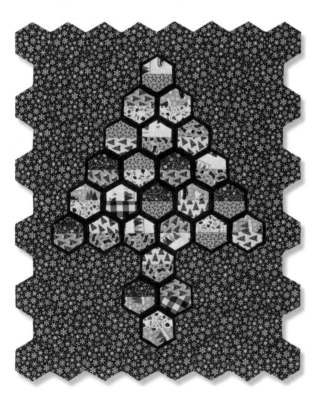

materials

PROJECT SIZE
36" x 42½"

BLOCK SIZE
2½" finished hexagon

PROJECT SUPPLIES
3 packages 5" print squares
Twin size batting
  (approximately 72" x 93")
1¾ yards accent fabric
1 yard green fabric

OTHER
Quilt As You Go 2½" Hexagon Set
  designed by Daisy & Grace for
  Missouri Star Quilt Company

SAMPLE PROJECT
Christmas Traditions by Dani Mogstad for
Riley Blake

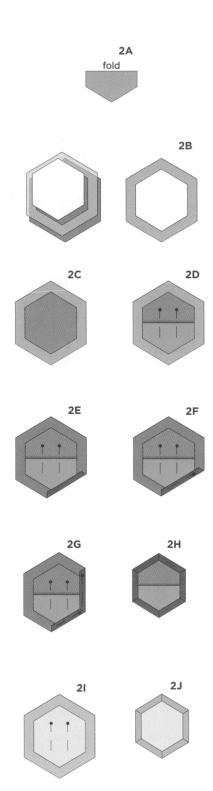

2A

fold

2B

2C   **2D**

2E   **2F**

2G   **2H**

2I   **2J**

1 sort & cut

From the green backing fabric, cut (5) 6″ strips across the width of the fabric. Cut large hexagons from the strips using the large hexagon template. Each strip will yield 6 large hexagons and a **total of 25** are needed.

From the backing accent fabric, cut (10) 6″ strips across the width of the fabric. Cut large hexagons from the strips using the large hexagon template. Each strip will yield 6 large hexagons and a **total of 58** are needed.

From the packages of 5″ print squares, select 50 green prints and 58 prints of other colors. Set the remaining 5″ squares aside for another project. Cut a small hexagon from each of the 5″ print squares using the small central hexagon template. A **total of 50** small green hexagons and a **total of 58** small print hexagons of other colors are needed.

From the batting, cut (6) 4½″ strips across the width of the batting. Using the small central hexagon template, cut small hexagons from the batting strips. Each strip will yield 14 small batting hexagons and a **total of 83** are needed. Set the remaining batting aside for another project.

2 method

From the 50 green print squares, choose 25 for your pocket fronts and fold each in half as shown, reverse sides facing. **2A**

Lay 1 large green hexagon on a flat surface wrong side up. Place the large hexagon template on top of the hexagon so that it lines up with it exactly. Place 1 batting hexagon into the recess within the template. **2B**

Place 1 small green hexagon right side up on top of the batting. **2C**

Place the folded pocket hexagon on top of the small green hexagon and pin in place. **2D**

Remove the large template. Fold 1 edge of the large hexagon to meet the edge of the central hexagon and finger press. **2E**

Fold the same edge over again so that it covers the raw edge of the central hexagon. Pin and slip stitch, but stop stitching just before the end, so you can carry on sewing once the next edge has been folded over. **Note:** If you prefer, you can machine topstitch the large backing hexagon close to the folded edge that overlaps the central hexagon. **2F**

Fold over the next edge, first to the central hexagon and then fold it again over the raw edge of the central hexagon (as done previously) to create mitered corner. **2G**

Keep folding and sewing around the hexagon until the entire hexagon is stitched. **Make 25** green pocket hexagons. **2H**

1 Choose 25 green print squares for your pocket fronts and fold each in half as shown, reverse sides facing.

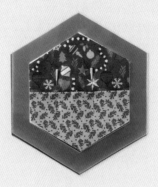

2 Lay 1 large green hexagon on a flat surface wrong side up. Place the large hexagon template on top of the hexagon, aligned with the edges. Place 1 batting hexagon and then a small green hexagon into the recess within the template. Place the folded pocket hexagon on top of the small green hexagon and pin in place.

3 Remove the template. Fold 1 edge of the large hexagon to meet the edge of the central hexagon and finger press. Fold the same edge over again so that it covers the raw edge of the central hexagon. Pin in place.

4 Fold over the next edge, as done previously, to create a mitered corner.

5 Keep folding and sewing around the hexagon until the entire hexagon is stitched. Make 25 green pocket hexagons.

6 Lay 1 large accent hexagon wrong side up. Place the large hexagon template on top of the hexagon, aligning edges. Place 1 batting hexagon and then 1 central print hexagon into the template recess. Repeat the steps in the method to make 58 print hexagons.

3A

Lay 1 large accent hexagon on a flat surface wrong side up. Place the large hexagon template on top of the hexagon so that it lines up with it exactly. Place 1 batting hexagon into the recess within the template. Place 1 central print hexagon right side up on top of the batting and pin in place. **2I**

Repeat the remaining steps in the method to bind the edges of the hexagon. **Make 58** print hexagons. **2J**

Block Size: 2½" finished hexagon

Note: Keep the construction method(s) consistent across your quilt—whether you hand sew, machine sew, or use a combination such as hand sewing the hexagons and machine stitching them together. Our projects were done by machine.

3 layout & finish

Turn each hexagon without a pocket face down. Arrange your completed hexagons in **11 rows** as shown, using a combination of the pocket hexagons face up and the non-pocket hexagons face down. Pay particular attention to the placement of the green pocket hexagons so that they form the tree and the pockets all open from the top. Use the diagrams to the left as needed. Each odd-numbered row will have **8 hexagons** and each even-numbered row will have **7 hexagons**. **3A**

Use a zigzag stitch or put back sides together and slip or ladder stitch blocks by hand to complete each row. Sew the rows together to complete the project.

Note: We have created numbered tags for your countdown to Christmas. You can download the free printable found at msqc.co/adventtags, or you can create your own tags. The tags can be taped or hole-punched and strung with ribbon to attach to the gifts. Stuff the pockets with notes, blessings, toys, or your favorite treats, add a tag, and count your way down to the holidays!

front

back

shown at 100%

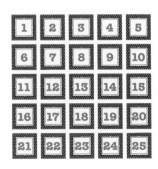

Ruby Sensation Sew-Along
PART 3

BLOCK ONLY

MATERIALS
BLOCK SIZE
12½" unfinished, 12" finished

DIAMOND PINWHEEL BLOCK
½ yard fabric A or (6) 2½" strips
½ yard fabric B or (6) 2½" strips
½ yard fabric D or (6) 2½" strips
1 yard background fabric

Note: Fabric C is not used in the block for Part Three.

FULL QUILT

MATERIALS
QUILT SIZE
86" x 86"

QUILT TOP
1¼ yards fabric A
1¼ yards fabric B
1½ yards fabric C
1¼ yards fabric D
5½ yards background fabric
  - includes inner border

OUTER BORDER
1½ yards

BINDING
¾ yard

BACKING
6¼ yards – vertical seam(s)
  or 2½ yards 108" wide

SAMPLE QUILT
Kona Solids Crimson, Chinese Red,
  Tomato, Sienna, White

FABRIC KEY	
■	A - Crimson
■	B - Chinese Red
■	C - Tomato
■	D - Sienna

DIAMOND PINWHEEL

1 cut

Note: Fabric C is not used in the Diamond Pinwheel blocks.

From each of the A, B, and D fabrics cut (2) 6½" strips across the width of the fabric. Subcut each strip into (16) 6½" x 2½" rectangles for a **total of 32** rectangles of each fabric.

Note: If you have chosen to use (6) 2½" strips each of A, B, and D, cut the strips into 6½" increments. Each strip will yield (6) 2½" x 6½" rectangles and a **total of 32** rectangles of each fabric are needed.

From the background fabric cut (12) 2½" strips across the width of the fabric. Subcut each strip into (16) 2½" squares for a **total of 192** background squares.

2 mark & sew

Mark a line from corner to corner once on the diagonal on the reverse side of each background square. **2A**

2A

Place a marked square atop a 6½" x 2½" fabric A rectangle as shown, right sides together. Sew on the marked line. Trim ¼" away from the sewn seam. Open and press toward the corner. **2B**

2B

Place a marked 2½" square atop the other end of the unit as shown, right sides together. Sew on the marked line. Trim

2C

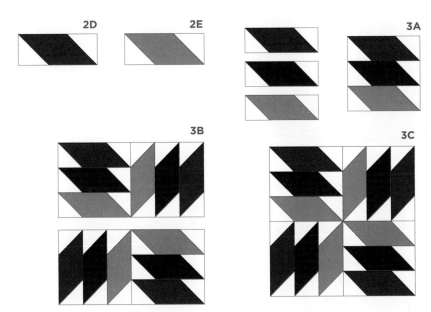

¼″ away from the sewn seam. Open and press toward the corner. **Make 32** A units. **2C**

Repeat to add background corners to both ends of each B rectangle for a **total of 32** B units. **2D**

Repeat to add background corners to both ends of each D rectangle for a **total of 32** D units. **2E**

3 block construction

Arrange a B, A, and D unit as shown. Sew the units together to make 1 quadrant. **Make 4**. **3A**

Arrange 4 quadrants as shown. Sew the quadrants together to form 2 rows. Press the seam of the top row to the right and the seam of the bottom row to the left. Nest the seams and sew the rows together to complete the block. **Make 8**. **3B 3C**

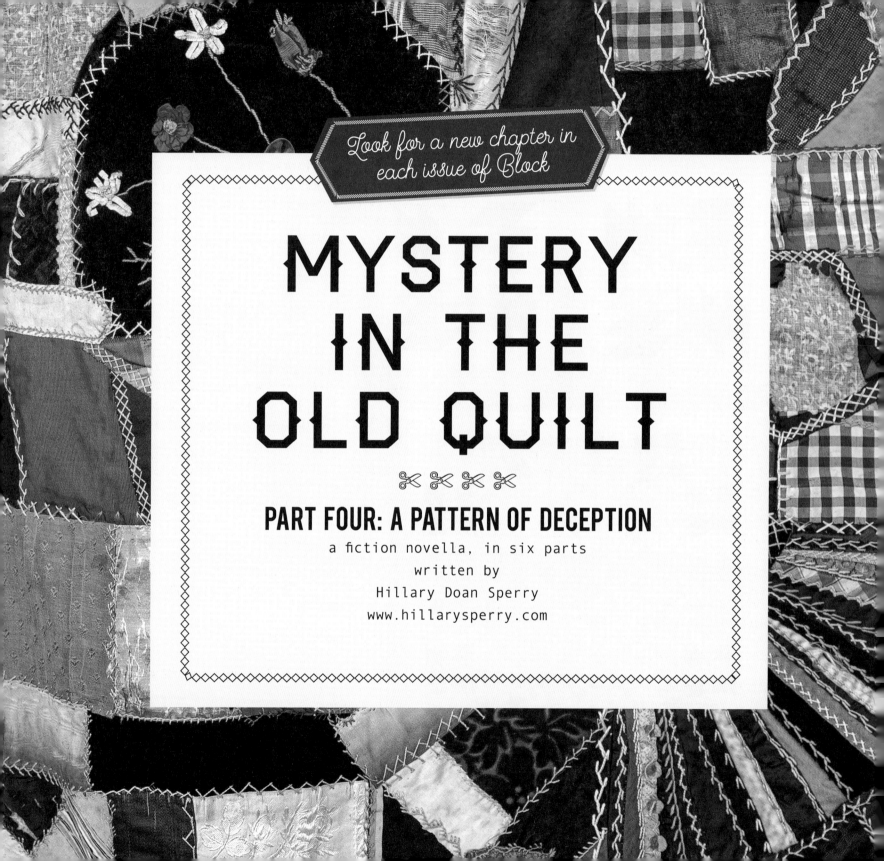

Look for a new chapter in each issue of Block

MYSTERY IN THE OLD QUILT

✄ ✄ ✄ ✄

PART FOUR: A PATTERN OF DECEPTION

a fiction novella, in six parts

written by

Hillary Doan Sperry

www.hillarysperry.com

"Don't touch that." Jenny swatted Officer Wilkins' hand from disrupting her freshly disorganized fabric squares. "I mean, please don't touch that. They're for a quilt I'm filming."

"Just checking things out." Officer Wilkins raised his hands in response and continued around the room while his partner, Officer Dunn, finished questioning Michelle.

The two officers had arrived shortly before Jenny had returned to her studio. Michelle had met them and while Officer Dunn questioned Jenny's assistant, Officer Wilkins circled the room looking through everything he could see.

Jenny spun a spool of thread between her fingers, anxiously waiting for the men to leave. It was bright red, the color of love . . . or irritation. The latter emotion pervaded the room, creating a cloud of anxiety around the little group. She tossed the thread in a drawer and looked back at the busy police officers. Officer Dunn pointed out the window toward the food truck owned and run by Michelle's family, the Peters.

"My boyfriend, Danny, works there with my dad and sometimes at the house," Michelle said, sounding exhausted. "My dad's remodeling the kitchen, and Danny is cheap labor, I guess."

Jenny was grateful Michelle's dad, Sam, had help. Although Ron had volunteered to help as well, after the break-ins and financial stress the struggling family needed some relief.

"How long have you and Danny been dating?" Officer Dunn asked.

Michelle put a hand to her forehead. "I don't know. Maybe, four months?"

"I see." Officer Dunn scribbled something, and Michelle's brow furrowed as she tried to catch what he was writing.

"Can't you tell him to ease up?" Jenny whispered to Officer Wilkins as he passed her desk. He raised an eyebrow and ignored her, moving toward the worktable in the center of the room. Jenny picked up her sketchbook, flipping to the quilt she should be working on, and tried to push down the automatic offense she had taken to his silence.

Officer Wilkins bent down, feeling under the edge of the worktable's lower shelf. He stood up and had a necklace dangling from his fingers. Michelle stopped talking, her attention fully on the little trinket in Officer Wilkins' hand.

"Can anyone vouch for your whereabouts this morning, Ms. Peters? Maybe your parents or Daniel?" Officer Dunn asked.

Michelle didn't hear him, her eyes were focused on Wilkins. She reached out, claiming the necklace he held. "That's mine."

"Ms. Peters? Your whereabouts?" Officer Dunn repeated.

Michelle pulled her focus back. "Sorry. I was here, in the studio. Jenny has a trip coming up, and I needed to finalize some things."

"Can anyone vouch for that?"

"My mother knows what time I left," Michelle said.

"So, no." Wilkins interjected. "And what about last night?"

"Blair's place was broken into this morning, not last night," Officer Dunn said, turning to his partner.

Officer Wilkins stepped closer and lowered his voice. "The Peters' food truck was broken into last night. Jenny was attacked. It would have made a great distraction for someone trying to take the quilt."

"But why?" Dunn looked perplexed and did his best to turn away from them, but Jenny could still hear.

"I don't know yet," Wilkins responded. He then turned to Michelle. "Have you had any struggles with Mrs. Doan?"

"Of course not."

"Do you know the value of the quilt that was stolen this morning?"

"Sure. My mother and I were talking about it yesterday. Jenny had mentioned that when it's finished Blair will get a pretty big inheritance."

"How big?" Wilkins pushed.

"I don't know . . . twenty-five, fifty thousand? But if she doesn't finish the quilt, all the money goes to charity." Michelle bit her lip.

"So, where were you last night?" Officer Wilkins stared Michelle down, and Jenny dug into a pile of fabric squares, sorting them for the third time and trying not to notice the tension stretching through the room.

"Danny canceled our date. I was at home with my parents. Need any other embarrassing details?" Michelle bit the words out.

Officer Wilkins didn't look away. He rapped his knuckles on the table and stepped closer. "That's interesting. So we don't know where Danny was last night or this morning? Was he there while you

were discussing the quilt's value with your mother?" Officer Wilkins asked.

Michelle's jaw dropped open, her head shaking slightly. "I don't know. Maybe?"

"I see." Officer Dunn stepped back, closing his notepad, "Thank you, ma'am. We very much appreciate your cooperation. Of course, we'll need to verify this, but thank you for your time."

Officer Wilkins turned to Jenny's desk before following his partner's lead. "Thank you for letting us look around."

"Anytime, officer." Jenny replied shortly.

Her tight response brought a smile to the officers' lips. "Relax. This will all work out." Officer Wilkins gave Jenny and Michelle a nod. "Oh, and you might want to tell your cleaning staff about the mess hanging out under that table."

"Excuse me. Our staff cleans very well, every night!" Michelle's offense was almost humorous.

Officer Wilkins paused, "Did they come before or after I was here last night?"

"Before. They're usually in about seven, after the stores close." Jenny assured him.

"Good to know." He winked and closed the door behind him.

"The nerve," Michelle said, getting down on her knees and fishing out a small pile of debris from the corner where he'd found Michelle's necklace. "A sticky note and a pearl button. Really? I wonder what we'd find at his house."

"A pearl button?" Jenny asked. She crossed the room to examine what Michelle had found.

Michelle sat down and hung the necklace around her throat, only to have it fall off again.

"Want me to help you?" Jenny asked, rolling the pearl button between her fingers. She had a lot of fabric and notions, but pearl buttons weren't on the list of quilting supplies she kept around very often. Michelle pulled the necklace off and shook her head.

"No, it must be my mother's. We have matching ones, but her clasp doesn't always stay together. I must have grabbed the wrong one."

Michelle reached out to drop the rest of the debris in the trash.

"Wait." Jenny reached to stop her. Gina Sloane's name was scrawled across the top of the little yellow sticky note. It was followed by key points about the quilt guild and Gina's memorial quilt. It looked like parts of the speech Loretta had given at the guild meeting. What was that doing here? She wondered. The button felt heavier in Jenny's hand.

"Loretta," Jenny whispered to herself. She could see the snagged cuff of Loretta's shirt with the missing pearl button. She glanced at the door where the police had left and carefully placed the note and button in her purse. Before she handed her suspicions over to someone who would tuck them into a back drawer, she wanted to talk with that woman.

***

Jenny pulled into Loretta's driveway and gathered her courage before approaching the door. When Loretta answered, Jenny gave her a big smile.

"Hi, Lo, how're you doing?"

Loretta puffed her chest out and examined Jenny.

"Fine. Why are you here?"

Jenny flinched and handed her a plate of cookies Ron had made, as a peace offering. "I was wondering how you were feeling. I could tell you were having a hard time after Gina's memorial quilt presentation." Loretta fumbled with the sleeve of her cuff. The button was still missing, and Jenny suspected the match was sitting in her pocket. She just needed to find out when and why Loretta had been in her studio.

Loretta fell back a step. "I don't know what you mean. Gina's passing was hard on everyone."

Tears welled in Loretta's eyes, and Jenny fumbled a little to get her footing. She reached out, taking Loretta's hand in her own. "It was, but you and Gina were so close."

Loretta held her breath, and suddenly tears leaked onto her cheeks. The grip of their clasped hands tightened and before Jenny realized what was happening, Loretta stepped back, inviting her inside.

"I didn't think anyone noticed." She brushed at her tears and indicated a high wingback chair for Jenny to sit in. "Gina was always so prompt and precise. Her quilting was beautiful, and she helped with the guild records. I couldn't believe it when she passed away."

"Yes, she was a very thorough woman." Jenny nodded, trying to come up with some interaction that illustrated the efficiency of Gina Sloane.

Then Loretta scowled. "Until she handed off that unfinished quilt to Blair. It was so unlike her."

continued on page 96

Easy Ways to Finish English Paper Piecing

Once you have your pretty little English paper pieces sewn together, what's next? Finishing EPP may seem daunting, but we're here to help you add the perfect finishing touch to your project! Whether you prefer to hand stitch or machine quilt, there are so many ways to make it yours.

First of all, when you're finished with your English paper piecing, pull the paper templates out "like a bandaid" as Sue Daley says. There's no need to be too dainty here. They'll pop right out. Save them if you'd like to use them again. Then, the next step depends on how you're finishing your project. There are many choices when it comes to finishing English paper pieced projects, but we've delved a little deeper into four different options to make your EPP project truly shine!

1. Straight Edges

If you want to quilt your project as you would a typical quilt, press your entire quilt top well without the papers inside, and prepare it to be basted to the batting and backing. You'll want to flatten the outer edges, instead of keeping them tucked under. They may not want to lay completely flat, but just do the best you can. At this point, some people prefer to trim off the points so that their quilt has a straight edge. If you choose to do this, simply follow our finishing instructions on page 110.

2. Pointed Edges

If you have kept your points on the edges, here are a couple tips to help you bind your quilt once it's been quilted. And, don't worry, it's much easier than you think! Prepare 2½" bias binding and trim the edges of your quilt, preserving the points. Bias binding is best here because it has a bit of stretch to help you make your way around the points easier. When you go to machine stitch on your binding, stitch slowly and on outside convex points, you'll need to fold your binding away from the quilt and then fold it back to align with the new edge, creating a small pleat or crease. Pin it in place and keep on stitching! For the inner concave points, take your time, straighten out the edge of the quilt, and keep on stitching. It's a cinch!

3. Machine Appliqué

If you have a bevy of unattached EPP blocks and would like to finish them with ease, consider machine appliquéing them onto background quilt blocks instead of attaching them all together. It's Jenny's favorite way to finish her EPP projects! That way, you

can easily join the blocks together, with or without sashing, and quilt as normal. To machine appliqué, all you need to do is glue baste your design right onto the backing and stitch it down. To learn more about machine appliqué, hop on over to page 58

4. Facing a Quilt

This way of finishing a quilt may not be well-known to you, but it's pretty marvelous! This method eliminates the need for binding while preserving the edge of your project without interrupting the flow of the design. Facing a quilt with straight edges is similar to binding. You simply cut double fold binding strips equal to the length of each side of the quilt, but don't join them together. Then, stitch each individual strip to the front of the quilt as usual, overlapping the top and bottom strips completely over the side strips (the side

strips can be a bit shorter). Once all of the strips are sewn onto the front of the quilt, flip them around to the back of the quilt and tuck the corners in, making sure the corners are still well-defined. Press the strips completely to the back and then stitch the bottom edge of your facing down onto your backing with an invisible stitch.

5. EPP Facing

If your EPP project does not have straight edges and you still want to face your quilt, in a manner, here's a fancy way to finish it. It may be a challenge for a larger project, but it's perfect for smaller table toppers and wall quilts. Create an EPP border of your entire project's outline. Join the shapes together to mirror the outside edge of your quilt. Do not flip the edges out on the front of your project or the back. Attach batting and backing to the back of your quilt, being sure to trim them so that they don't quite reach the edge of your project, and quilt as usual. Then, once your project is entirely quilted, machine stitch or hand stitch the border of finished EPP blocks to the front of your quilt with the right sides facing. When you're finished sewing the border onto the front, flip it to the back, being sure to carefully reshape the points. Press well! Finally, stitch the back edge of your border down onto the backing.

Finishing an English paper piecing project does require a bit of finesse, but the result is well worth it! We hope your project turns out beautifully. Share your results with us at #msqcshowandtell. We would be delighted to see what you've been working on.

For the tutorial and everything you need to make this quilt visit:
www.msqc.co/Blockv7issue4

Happy Accidents
Diamond Terrace Quilt

Things don't always go according to plan. That's true in life; that's true in quilting. The key is to remain positive. Look for good! Because sometimes those hiccups teach valuable lessons. (Note to self: Keep fingers far from moving needles!) And sometimes your "mistake" turns out even better than the best-laid plan! After all, quilting is a journey, and a wrong turn just might become the best part of the adventure!

Six years ago, Maren and Henry Simpson were preparing to leave their home and family to spend a year in another state as volunteers for their church. Knowing how hard it would be to leave their seven children and twenty-two grandchildren, a sweet daughter-in-law got to work on a special family quilt.

Alisa began by piecing basic pinwheels in blue and white. Then, she cut large white squares and hand-embroidered a center block featuring Maren and Henry's names below the outline of the place they had been married almost fifty years earlier. Matching quilt blocks were embroidered for each of the grown children and their spouses.

Next, she embroidered tracings of the grandchildren's handprints and names, each in their favorite color. Yellow for Davey, purple for Cora, and pale pink for Jane, the youngest granddaughter.

When the hand work was complete, Alisa spread thirty pinwheels and thirty embroidered blocks on the family room floor to plan her layout. She arranged and rearranged, but nothing looked quite right!

Finally, she settled on a less-than-ideal solution: She cut two blocks of white background fabric, left them plain—no embroidery at all—and placed them in the top two corners. Those blocks would be hidden by pillows anyway, she reasoned.

When Henry and Maren arrived at their "home away from home," the quilt was spread over their new bed. Night after night, they slept under that beautiful symbol of family.

The weeks turned into months, and before long, Maren and Henry had completed their church service. They returned home to the same sweet faces they had left a year earlier, though some had grown an inch or two.

And then, a funny thing happened. Maren discovered her family tree was about to expand by not one, but two new grandbabies! A baby boy was born at Christmastime, and a little girl followed just before Easter.

It seems those two blank spaces were meant to be. Alisa gathered her needle and thread and stitched a tiny handprint in each empty block.

Finally, the family was complete, and so was the quilt.

materials

QUILT SIZE
90" x 95"

BLOCK SIZE
8 x 10½" unfinished, 7½" x 10" finished

QUILT TOP
1 roll 2½" print strips
4 yards background fabric
  - includes inner border

OUTER BORDER
1¾ yards

BINDING
¾ yard

BACKING
8½ yards - vertical seam(s)
  or 3 yards of 108" wide

SAMPLE QUILT
Bloomington by Lella Boutique
for Moda Fabrics

1 cut

From each of the 2½" print strips, cut (10) 2½" x 4" rectangles. Organize these rectangles in groups of 5 cut from the same fabric.

From the background fabric, cut (55) 2½" strips. Set 8 of the strips aside for the inner border.

- From 27 of the strips, subcut 2½" x 4½" rectangles. Each strip will yield 9 rectangles and a **total of 240** are needed.

- From 20 of the strips, subcut 2½" squares. Each strip will yield 16 squares and a **total of 320** are needed.

2 sew

Pick up a set of (5) 2½" x 4" print rectangles, (3) 2½" x 4½" background rectangles, and (4) 2½" background squares.

Sew a 2½" x 4½" background rectangle to the right side of a print rectangle. **Make 3** A units. **2A**

Sew a 2½" background square to both short ends of a print rectangle. **Make 2** B units. **2B**

Arrange the 5 units as shown, alternating between A and B units. The A unit in the center is rotated 180° from the way it was sewn. Sew the units together to form a block and press the seams toward

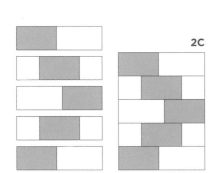

the bottom of the block. **Make 80** blocks and keep all of the blocks made from the same print fabrics organized together. **2C**

Block Size: 8" x 10½" unfinished, 7½" x 10" finished

3 arrange & sew

Use the diagram on page 49 to lay out the blocks in **8 rows** of **10 blocks**. Make note of the arrangement and orientation of the blocks as most of them are paired with a block of matching fabric forming a diamond shape.

Sew the blocks together to form rows. Press the seams of the odd-numbered rows to the left and the seams of the even-numbered rows to the right. Sew the rows together and press to complete the quilt center.

4 inner border

Pick up the (8) 2½" background strips set aside earlier and sew them together end-to-end to make 1 long strip. Trim the inner borders from this strip.

Refer to Borders (pg. 110) in the Construction Basics to measure, cut, and attach the borders. The strips are approximately 80½" for the sides and approximately 79½" for the top and bottom.

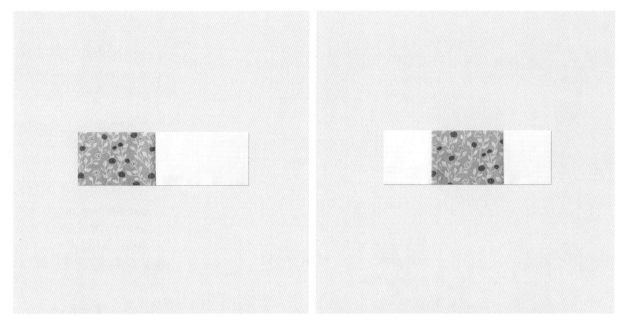

1   Sew a 2½" x 4½" background rectangle to the right side of a print rectangle and press toward the darker fabric. Make 3 A units.

2   Sew a 2½" background square to each short end of a print rectangle. Make 2 B units.

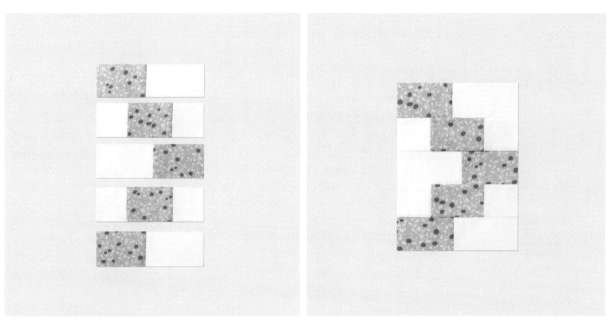

3   Arrange the 3 A units and 2 B units as shown. Notice the A unit in the center is rotated 180°.

4   Sew the units together to form a block.

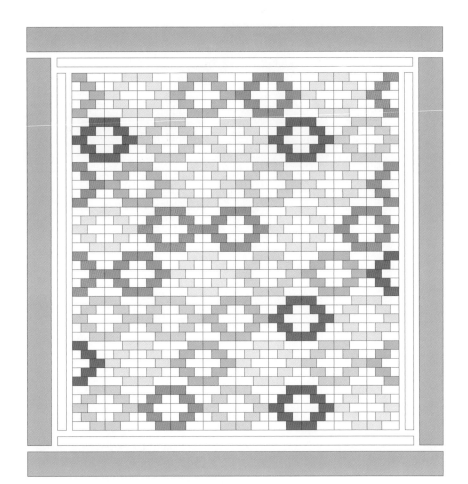

5 outer border

From the outer border fabric, cut (9) 6″ strips across the width of the fabric. Sew the strips together end-to-end to make 1 long strip. Trim the outer borders from this strip.

Refer to Borders (pg. 110) in the Construction Basics to measure, cut, and attach the borders. The strips are approximately 84½″ for the sides and approximately 90½″ for the top and bottom.

6 quilt & bind

Layer the quilt with batting and backing and quilt. After the quilting is complete, square up the quilt and trim away all excess batting and backing. Add binding to complete the quilt. See Construction Basics (pg. 110) for binding instructions.

For the tutorial and everything you need to make this quilt visit:
www.msqc.co/Blockv7issue4

Halloween All Year Long

Trick or Treat Street Table Runner

What's your favorite holiday? There are so many that we get to enjoy throughout the year, but there's always that one holiday that holds a special place in our hearts. I can tell you I know plenty of people who would keep their Christmas tree up year 'round if it was socially acceptable, which it certainly should be! I know of one young lady who celebrates her favorite holiday year all year long. Halloween!

I met Janie when she worked in Sew Seasonal. I'd first met her when I popped into the shop for some fabric I needed for an upcoming tutorial. After introducing ourselves I asked her how she was enjoying her job, to which she responded with a giant grin, "Oh, you have no idea! I'm so happy I'm here." Considering the skeleton pin grinning up at me from Janie's apron, I should have guessed what it was about the shop she was so excited about. But I still smiled and asked, "Really? Why is that?" Janie gestured toward a shelf of fabric and threw her arms open in an enthusiastic "Ta-da" gesture and said, "Halloween fabric, Miss Jenny!" Janie's excitement gave me a good giggle, but I learned quickly just how much this girl loved everything Halloween.

Janie fully embraced the shop's seasonal theme, but it was clear which holiday was number one for her. The shop music was always a consistent playlist of soundtracks from movies like *Harry Potter*, *The Nightmare Before Christmas*, and pretty much every piece of music composed by

Danny Elfman. Janie also liked to proudly display her love for Halloween. Each time I saw her, she had a new Halloween themed pin on her apron, and she'd always have her hair pulled back with a bow she made from a scrap of Halloween fabric! Janie's enthusiasm for Halloween showed especially when she was helping guests in the shop. Anytime someone came in looking for Halloween fabric, Janie would prance to the Halloween section and proudly list every collection in stock. Janie proved to be just as great a customer as she was an employee because sometimes she'd wind up shopping with the guests!

Each time a new shipment of Halloween fabric was dropped off at the shop, Janie was the first one unboxing the bolts and spying which ones she wanted cut for herself. Now I firmly believe a quilter never needs an excuse to buy fabric, but considering how far away the spooky season was at the time, I had to ask Janie what she planned to do with all the fabric she was buying. She eagerly plopped two big cuts of black fabric out on the counter, each printed with elegant white and orange pumpkins, and said, "I'm going to turn these into curtains for my bedroom window."

"Halloween curtains? Now? In April?"

Janie nodded, "Yes, ma'am! Every day is Halloween for me."

materials

PROJECT SIZE
40" x 30"

BLOCK SIZE
10½" unfinished, 10" finished

PROJECT TOP
1 package 5" print squares
½ yard yellow solid fabric
 - includes inner border
¾ yard gray background fabric

BORDER
¾ yard

BINDING
½ yard

BACKING
1 yard

OTHER
Missouri Star Large Dresden Plate
 Template for 10" squares
¾ yard fusible web

SAMPLE QUILT
Ghosts and Ghouls by Stacy Iest Hsu
for Moda Fabrics

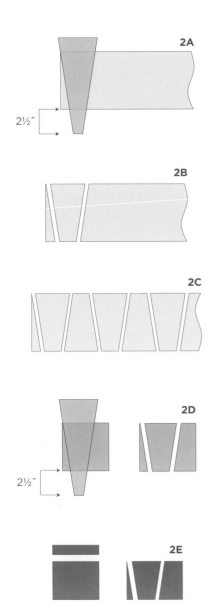

2A

2½"

2B

2C

2D

2½"

2E

1 cut

From the gray background fabric, cut (2) 10½" strips across the width of the fabric. Subcut (6) 10½" squares. Set the remaining fabric aside for another project.

From the yellow solid fabric, cut (1) 6" strip across the width of the fabric. Set the remaining fabric aside for the inner border.

2 make houses

Note: You can vary the number of 6", 5", and 4" tall houses for your project. You just need a **total of 30** Dresden houses. Have fun and make it your own!

Lay the 6" yellow strip on your cutting surface horizontally. Place the Dresden template on top of the strip as shown, lining up the 2½" mark of the template with the bottom edge of the strip. **2A**

Carefully cut along both sides of the template. **2B**

Turn the template 180°, lining up the left edges and the 2½" mark of the template with the top of the strip. Cut another Dresden. Continue in this fashion to **cut 5** yellow Dresdens from the strip. Set the remaining piece of the strip aside for the appliqué shapes. **2C**

Select (25) 5" print squares with varying prints to use for houses.

Stack as many squares on your cutting surface as you feel comfortable cutting at 1 time and align all edges. Lay the template along 1 side of the squares and line up the 2½" mark of the template with the bottom edge of the squares. Carefully cut along both sides of the template. **2D**

Cut (13) 5" print Dresdens. Set the scraps aside for the appliqué shapes.

Trim 1" from the top of each of the 12 remaining squares. The 1" strip can be set aside for the appliqué windows. Repeat the previous instructions to **cut (12)** 4" print Dresdens from the trimmed squares. **2E**

Select (2) 4" and (2) 5" Dresdens of varying prints. Add 1 yellow Dresden and arrange so there are Dresdens of different heights next to each other. When you are pleased with your arrangement, sew the Dresdens together using a ¼" seam allowance. The small end of the Dresdens should always be lined up. Press the seam allowances toward the tallest Dresdens. Where the top edges of the tallest Dresdens extend past the shorter Dresdens, turn the raw edges under ¼" and press. **2F**

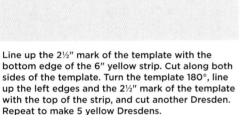

1 Line up the 2½" mark of the template with the bottom edge of the 6" yellow strip. Cut along both sides of the template. Turn the template 180°, line up the left edges and the 2½" mark of the template with the top of the strip, and cut another Dresden. Repeat to make 5 yellow Dresdens.

2 Lay the template along 1 side of the 5" squares and line up the 2½" mark of the template with the bottom edge of the squares. Carefully cut along both sides of the template. Cut (13) 5" print Dresdens.

3 Trim 1" from the top of each of 12 print squares. Repeat the previous instructions to cut (12) 4" print Dresdens from the trimmed squares.

4 Arrange 1 yellow Dresden, (2) 4" Dresdens, and (2) 5" Dresdens so there are different heights next to each other. Sew them together using a ¼" seam allowance, aligning the small ends. Press toward the tallest Dresdens and turn any remaining raw edges under ¼" and press.

5 Lay the Dresden unit atop a 10½" background square and pin in place or attach with spray adhesive.

6 Arrange and adhere the doors and windows, then stitch around the edges of the appliqué shapes and along the bottom edge of the houses with a blanket or zigzag stitch.

2F

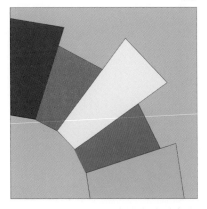

2G

Lay the Dresden unit atop a 10½"
background square as shown. Pin in place
or attach with spray adhesive. **2G**

Repeat the previous steps to **make 6**
blocks. **Note:** 1 block will have 5 print
Dresdens and no yellow Dresden.

3 appliqué windows & doors

Note: The templates we used to
create the bats, roofs, doors, and
windows are available for download at
msqc.co/treatstreettemplate. The
template shapes are meant to be a
starting point. Feel free to modify them to
your liking or create your own shapes.

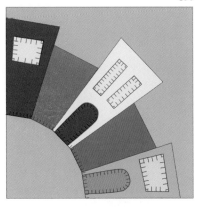

3A

For each appliqué shape needed, trace
the appropriate template onto the paper
side of your fusible web. Roughly cut
around the traced line and then follow the
manufacturer's instructions to adhere the
fusible web to the reverse side of your
fabric. Use the remaining 5" print squares
and any leftover pieces set aside earlier
to create your shapes. Once the fusible
web has adhered, carefully cut along the
traced line. Peel off the paper backing
and discard it.

Note: For this step, you will be
appliquéing doors and windows only. The
roofs and bats will be appliquéd after the
borders are added.

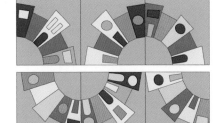

4A

Once you have prepared each of the
shapes needed for your block, lay
them out on top of the block. Make any
modifications or adjustments you like. Do
not place windows or doors within the ¼"
seam allowance along the outer edges.
When you're happy with the arrangement,
follow the manufacturer's instructions to
adhere the shapes to the block.

After all of the appliqué windows and
doors have been fused to the block, stitch
around the edges of the appliqué shapes
and along the bottom edge of the houses
with a blanket or zigzag stitch. **3A**

Block Size: 10½" unfinished, 10" finished

4 arrange & sew

Referring to the diagram **4A**, lay out your
blocks in **2 rows** of **3 blocks** each. Pay
special attention to the orientation of the
blocks. Sew the blocks together in rows.
Press the seam allowances of the top
row to the left and the bottom row to
the right. Nest the seams and sew the
rows together. Press the seam towards
the bottom.

5 inner border

Cut (3) 1½" strips across the width of the
yellow fabric set aside earlier. Trim the
borders from these strips.

Refer to Borders (pg. 110) in the
Construction Basics to measure, cut,
and add the inner borders. The strips
are approximately 30½" for the top and

bottom and approximately 22½" for the sides. **Note:** The top and bottom strips are sewn on first, followed by the side strips for this project.

6 outer border

Cut (4) 4½" strips across the width of the outer border fabric. Trim the borders from these strips.

Refer to Borders (pg. 110) in the Construction Basics to measure, cut, and add the outer borders. The strips are approximately 32½" for the top and bottom and approximately 30½" for the sides. **Note:** The top and bottom strips are sewn on first, followed by the side strips for this project.

7 appliqué roofs & bats

Following the instructions outlined in section 3—trace, fuse, and cut out the shapes needed for your roofs and bats from fabrics that will provide contrast to the borders and the houses to which they are applied.

Referring to the diagram on page 57 as needed, lay the shapes on top of your project top. Make any modifications or adjustments you like. When you're happy with the arrangement, follow the manufacturer's instructions to adhere the shapes to the project top.

After all of the appliqué shapes have been fused to the top, stitch around any remaining raw edges of your project with a blanket or zigzag stitch.

8 quilt & bind

Layer the table runner with batting and backing and quilt. After the quilting is complete, square up the project and trim away all excess batting and backing. Add binding to complete the project. See Construction Basics (pg. 110) for binding instructions.

Find a BONUS Christmas version of
this in your digital copy of BLOCK

Have Fun With Fusible Appliqué

Start off on the Right Foot

Be sure to change out your sewing machine foot before you start appliquéing. An open toe appliqué foot has a wider space in the middle and is often made of clear plastic so you can see what you're sewing with ease.

Fusible appliqué hasn't always been my friend. I remember those early days trying to figure it out on my own and, believe me, it wasn't too pretty. But as time has gone on, I've picked up a few tips and tricks to make it fun! Keep reading to learn more about fusible machine appliqué. My good friend, Courtenay Hughes, who teaches many of our wonderful in-town classes, has offered some of her advice to help your projects come together beautifully!

Supplies Needed:

Templates	Iron
Sewing machine needle	Teflon Pressing Sheet
Thread	Small, sharp scissors
Fabric	Open toe appliqué foot for
Heat n Bond Lite	your sewing machine
or Lite Steam-A-Seam 2	

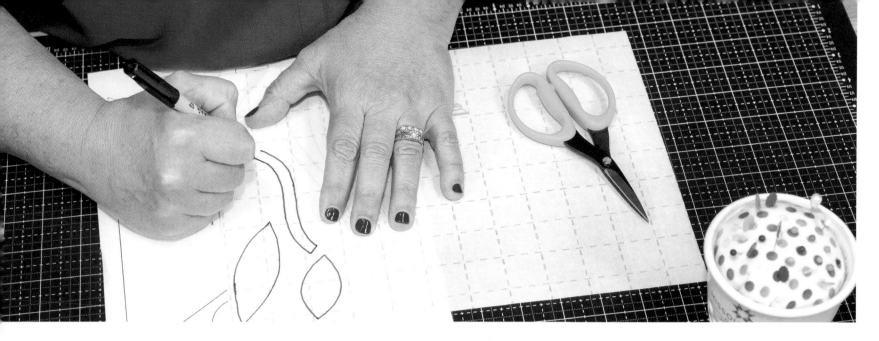

Preparing Paper for Appliqué Shapes

One of the first things to keep in mind when getting your shapes ready for appliqué is whether or not to reverse them. If the individual shapes are symmetrical, there is no need to reverse them, but if the shapes are asymmetrical, be sure to turn them over to the wrong side and trace them onto your fusible with a light box or a window. That means the shape on the fusible will be facing the right direction. Hurray! Then, you take your shapes and trace them directly onto the paper side of the fusible you're using. Then they are ready to be ironed on to the wrong side of the fabric.

Cutting Fabric Shapes

Once your shapes are traced onto the paper side of the fusible, you are ready to cut them out. Use a small, sharp pair of scissors and leave about ⅛ to ¼ inch around the outside of the shape. Don't cut right on the line just yet! After you iron it onto the fabric is when you'll actually cut on the line.

Stay Sharp!

We recommend changing out your sewing machine needle to an 80-12 microtex. It's a slimmer needle with an extra sharp point that's ideal for piecing and appliquéing alike.

When you go to fuse your shapes onto the fabric, pay attention to the direction of the print and the design of the fabric. This is an opportunity for a bit of fussy cutting if you want to get fancy. Center a cute motif for a decorative touch or match a directional print to really make part of the design stand out.

Appliquéing Shapes to Fabric

Follow the manufacturer's directions to adhere them to the fabric; some types of fusible require heat and some don't. Then cut your shapes out on the line with a sharp pair of scissors. Now they're ready to arrange and fuse on your quilt block. Pay attention to the order of the shapes on the block as you are fusing them. It may help to number the pieces to know in which order to fuse them. If your design has layers, start with the bottom layer and work your way to the top layer. And if your layout isn't picture perfect, guess what? That's okay! It's your own unique design.

Sewing points, curves, circles, and layers

Before you stitch your fused pieces of fabric down, test the stitch you'd like to use and adjust it to your liking. Some people prefer a wider zigzag stitch, some like it narrow. It's up to you! It just needs to be big enough to stitch down the edge of the fabric. Try to choose a stitch length and width that works for all pieces in your project, so don't go too big if you have smaller pieces.

And here's an important reminder: when you find the setting you like, write it down or take a picture of it with your phone so you don't forget it! As for thread color, using thread that matches your design is more forgiving for those just starting out.

Right as you start sewing, pull enough thread out of your machine so you can hold on to your thread tails. Begin in a less conspicuous place with the needle down, preferably on a straight edge, not on the rounded part of a curve or the top of a point. Keep in mind, your stitch should just barely hit the background fabric. Stitch slowly and keep both hands on your project to guide it. Always pivot when your needle is on the outside edge. If you pivot before,

What's the Stitch?

Start out with 50wt cotton thread that matches your project when you begin. When you feel more comfortable, consider changing up the look of your appliqué by using a blanket stitch with a thicker 40wt thread in a contrasting or variegated color. For the bottom thread, try to always match your backing for a consistent look.

you'll create a v-shaped gap in the stitching. You may have to stop and start many times when you sew around a curve. Take it nice and easy. When you're stitching up to a point, sew right up to it and put your needle down at the tip of the point to make sure it's sewn down completely, then pivot and continue sewing. If your machine doesn't have a needle up/down function, just use your hand wheel to position your needle down before you start and stop.

When you're finished sewing a portion of your design and you need to stop, pull out nice long threads again and then clip them. You'll want to keep them long enough so you can bury them when you're finished. To bury your threads, simply thread both of the top threads into a needle (self-threading needles work great here), pull them through to the back, and tie them off. If you don't want dark threads to show through on lighter fabric, use your needle to weave your thread ends into the zigzag stitch on the back and trim them off.

Now, if you made a little boo boo and your threads are too short to tie off, just squeeze on a dot of fray check and they won't come loose. With this method, there's no need to backstitch and add unsightly bulk to your neat appliqué stitch. That's it. You're all finished! If you want to dig a little deeper into machine applique, take a look at this hour-long class "Beginning Machine Applique" taught by Courtenay Hughes, one of our wonderful quilting teachers!

Zig When They Zag

Using a zigzag stitch is simpler than a dense satin stitch for a beginner. It's easier to get good results with this stitch because you can control it with less effort. And using the needle up/down function helps as well. Stop with the needle down so you can pivot without losing your place.

Graduation Quilts for Three Granddaughters

I have three kind, capable, and intelligent granddaughters who graduated from high school this year. I'm so proud of them! Each is totally unique and her own person, so I made three different quilts for their three fun personalities. Congratulations girls! I love you so!

Hello Quilters!

I like to remind myself, "When the going gets tough, the tough get quilting!" and that's exactly what I've been up to lately. Despite the many challenges in this world, I know this is not the time to focus on the difficulties in my own life, but to look beyond myself and see how I can reach out. There are too many people who feel isolated and lonely right now and I have realized that quilting can be a lifeline—not just for those who receive our gifts, but also for those who create. It goes both ways. I hope you know how meaningful your contributions are in this world. You are all worthy of love and respect. I am so glad to call myself a quilter and know that we can do so much good together.

Jenny

2020 Senior Class Quilts

This has been a challenging year for our graduating seniors as they had not been able to attend class at school due to the Covid-19 outbreak. So, Natalie had the brilliant idea to make ALL our seniors quilts and literally wrap them with love and support! With the help of our amazing sewing team, we were able to stitch up 65 quilts for the entire senior class. We congratulate the Penney High School 2020 graduates and wish them the best of luck with their future endeavors! We have a feeling they'll go on to do wonderful things in this world.

For the tutorial and everything you need to make this project visit:
www.msqc.co/Blockv7issue4

One Scrap at a Time
Mini Double Nine-Patch Quilt

Life on the American frontier was hard. There were prairies to tame, trees to fell, and fences to build. There was butter to churn, laundry to scrub, and water to fetch.

Such labor-filled days didn't leave much time for quilting, but that didn't stop bitter winter winds from whipping across the plains and right through the logs of humble one-room cabins. Quilts weren't a luxury; they were a necessity of life.

So, in the midst of carding wool and boiling homemade soap, those resourceful pioneer women found ways to stitch fabric scraps into simple block quilts that were used not only as bed coverings, but as windows, room dividers, and doors, too.

Before this time, block quilts did exist, but they weren't common. Most patchwork quilts were created by adding pieces to an ever-growing whole, as in a medallion quilt. But as it usually is, necessity was the mother of invention. Block quilts were easier to make. They came together quickly and were less cumbersome and more portable. Of course, their primary purpose was warmth, not beauty, and yet, many of these utilitarian blocks are still beloved today.

One of the most popular pioneer-era blocks was the 9-Patch. This easy block was an excellent use for scraps, and since it was so simple, it was often the first pattern used to teach very young children how to quilt. I love to imagine a nineteenth-century child sitting at the knee of her mother as they both work with needle and thread to create warmth and comfort for their family.

Over the years, quilters have created countless variations of this historic block, including the beautifully intricate Mini Double Nine-Patch.

During the 1800s, fabric was scarce—so scarce that every precious scrap was saved for quilts. Patterns like the Double Nine-Patch transformed all those pieces into true works of art. Originally, Double Nine-Patch quilts were hand stitched one itty-bitty scrap at a time, but now we use quick and easy strip sets. (Thank goodness!)

As you make this pretty pattern, take a moment to remember those early American quilters whose ingenuity forever transformed the art of quilt making.

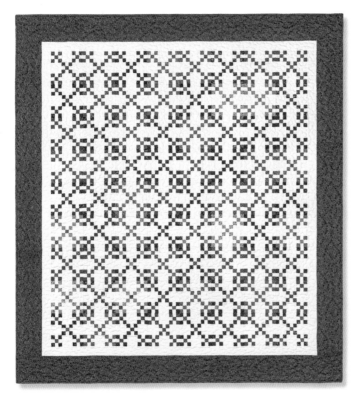

materials

QUILT SIZE
69" x 75¾"

BLOCK SIZE
7¼" unfinished, 6¾" finished

QUILT TOP
1 roll 2½" print strips
1 roll 2½" background strips
  - includes inner border
1¾ yards background fabric

OUTER BORDER
1¼ yards

BINDING
¾ yard

BACKING
4¾ yards - vertical seam(s)
  or 2½ yards of 108" wide

SAMPLE QUILT
October Morning by Kim Diehl for Henry Glass

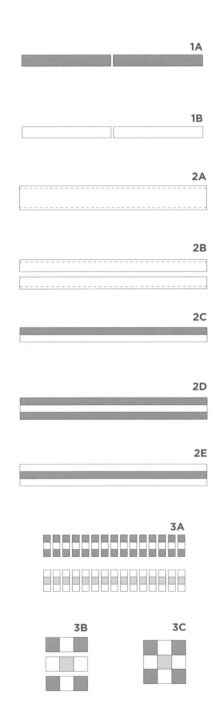

1A

1B

2A

2B

2C

2D

2E

3A

3B   3C

1 cut

Cut (30) 2½" print strips in half on the fold to yield a **total of (60)** 2½" strips that measure approximately 20-22" in length. Keep the matching halves of print strips together and set all remaining print strips aside for another project. **1A**

Cut (24) 2½" background strips in half on the fold to yield a **total of (48)** 2½" strips that measure approximately 20-22" in length. Set 6 of the remaining full-length background strips aside for the inner border. Set the rest of the strips aside for another project. **1B**

From the background fabric, cut (21) 2¾" strips across the width of the fabric. Subcut each strip into 2¾" squares. Each strip will yield 14 squares and a **total of 288** are needed.

2 make strip sets

Pick up a pair of matching print strips and 2 background strips. Lay 1 of the background strips atop 1 of the print strips, right sides together. Sew the strips together along both long edges to form a tube. **2A**

Cut the tube in half lengthwise, parallel to your sewn seams to yield 2 strip sets. Press the seam of each strip set toward the darker fabric. **2B 2C**

Cut the other matching print strip in half lengthwise to yield (2) 1¼" strips. Sew a 1¼" print strip to the strip set as shown. Press toward the darker fabric. **2D**

Make 48 print/background/print strip sets. Each print/background/print strip set should have a matching strip set.

Lay a background strip atop a print strip, right sides together. Sew the strips together along both long edges to form a tube. **Make 12** tubes. Cut each tube in half lengthwise to yield a **total of 24** strip sets. **2A 2B**

Cut the 12 remaining background strips in half lengthwise to yield a **total of (24)** 1¼" wide strips. Sew a 1¼" background strip to each strip set as shown. Press toward the darker fabric. **Make 24** background/print/background strip sets. **2E**

3 make small nine-patches

Cut each strip set into (15) 1¼" segments. Keep all matching segments together. A **total of 720** print/background/print segments are needed and we will refer to these as A units. A **total of 360** background/print/background segments are needed and we will refer to these as B units. **3A**

Pick up 10 matching A units and 5 matching B units. The prints within your chosen A and B units should not be the same fabric. Lay out 2 A units and 1 B unit as shown. Arrange the selected 3-patches as shown. **3B**

Nest the seams and sew the rows together to form a small 9-patch. Press the seams toward the bottom. **3C**

Use the rest of your selected A and B units to make a set of 5 matching small 9-patch units. Keep these units together to easily organize into blocks later on.

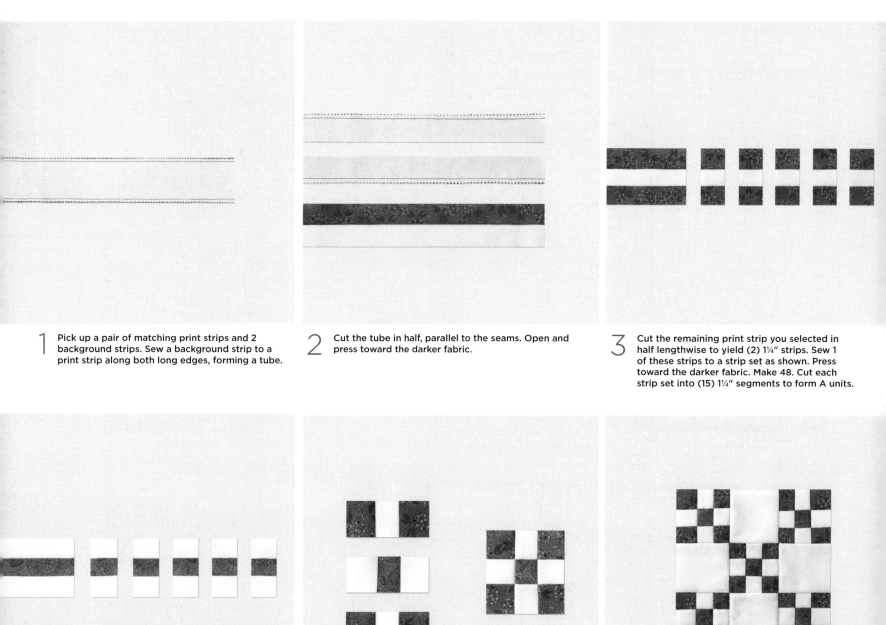

1   Pick up a pair of matching print strips and 2 background strips. Sew a background strip to a print strip along both long edges, forming a tube.

2   Cut the tube in half, parallel to the seams. Open and press toward the darker fabric.

3   Cut the remaining print strip you selected in half lengthwise to yield (2) 1¼" strips. Sew 1 of these strips to a strip set as shown. Press toward the darker fabric. Make 48. Cut each strip set into (15) 1¼" segments to form A units.

4   Cut 12 background strips in half lengthwise to yield 1¼" strips. Sew 1 strip to a strip set as shown. Press toward the darker fabric. Make 24. Cut each strip set into (15) 1¼" segments to form B units.

5   Lay out 2 matching A units and 1 B unit as shown. Sew the units together to form a 9-patch. Make (5) matching 9-patches for each block.

6   Arrange 5 matching 9-patches and (4) 2¾" background squares as shown. Sew the pieces together to form rows. Press toward the background squares. Nest the seams and sew the rows together to complete the block. Make 72 blocks.

Repeat to make 72 sets of 5 matching small 9-patches for a **total of 360** small 9-patches.

4 block construction

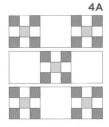

4A

Pick up a matching set of 5 small 9-patches and (4) 2¾" background squares. Arrange them into 3 rows of 3 and sew the units together to form rows. Press the seams toward the background squares. **4A**

Sew the rows together. Press the seams toward the bottom to complete the block. **Make 72** blocks. **4B**

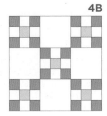

4B

Block Size: 7¼" unfinished, 6¾" finished

5 arrange & sew

Arrange the blocks into **9 rows** of **8 blocks** as shown in the diagram below. Sew the blocks together to form the rows. Press the seams

of the odd-numbered rows to the right and the seams of the even-numbered rows to the left. Sew the rows together to complete the center of the quilt.

6 inner border

Pick up the (6) 2½" background strips set aside earlier. Sew the strips together end-to-end to make 1 long strip. Trim the borders from this strip.

Refer to Borders (pg. 110) in the Construction Basics to measure, cut, and attach the borders. The strips are approximately 61¼" for the sides and approximately 58½" for the top and bottom.

7 outer border

Cut (7) 6" strips across the width of the outer border fabric. Sew the strips together end-to-end to make 1 long strip. Trim the borders from this strip.

Refer to Borders (pg. 110) in the Construction Basics to measure, cut, and attach the borders. The strips are approximately 65¼" for the sides and approximately 69½" for the top and bottom.

8 quilt & bind

Layer the quilt with batting and backing and quilt. After the quilting is complete, square up the quilt and trim away all excess batting and backing. Add binding to complete the quilt. See Construction Basics (pg. 110) for binding instructions.

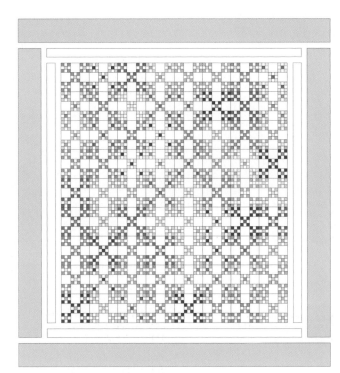

For the tutorial and everything you need to make this quilt visit:
www.msqc.co/Blockv7issue4

72

My Sister's Gift
Jenny's Easy Carpenter's Star Quilt

"My sister, Bonnie, was a single, cat-loving, direct redhead. Some would think she seemed cold, but down deep was a warm, loving human being. One comment at her funeral was that she was the nicest woman with 'teeth.'

"Bonnie, took a quilting class 30 years ago. It was a sampler quilt—each block was a different pattern. That was her introduction to quilting. She quickly tired of the unfinished sampler quilt and wanted to choose fabrics and patterns that suited her. Did I mention she was fiercely independent? She then moved on to new patterns and relished choosing the perfect fabric. Often, I was a part of the hunt for just the right fabric for these quilts. At the time, it made no sense to me to invest in fabric, cut it up and sew back together for a blanket.

"She continued making quilts. She also became adventurous in her color selections. She blossomed, choosing beautiful color palettes and patterns. Some were given away to friends, but most she kept. She would lay them on her spare room bed and called them her children. They were a tribute to her quilt journey from beginning to end.

"In 2014, Bonnie was diagnosed with neuroendocrine pancreatic cancer. We were told it was slow growing and her health journey began. I was blessed to be on this journey with her. She had monthly appointments at a medical facility far from home. It was during those car rides we talked a lot about family, work, life, and death. We also talked a lot about quilts, colors, patterns, fabric, and anything sewing-related. These discussions lit a spark in me.

"We would stop at fabric stores on the way to and from doctor appointments and on short weekend trips. She taught me the cutting process, and the quarter inch seam. Bonnie's motto was 'go big or go home.' So, we embarked on this huge pink pinwheel monstrosity just for me. Whew! It was hard to get those pinwheels spinning in the right direction, but Bonnie guided me through it. I gained confidence and she was proud of my work.

"Sadly, a month shy of her 59th birthday, my sister passed away. All the retirement dreams of travel, fun, and quilting were just that, dreams. As I went through her sewing room, I found a partially finished advent calendar, quilts in need of binding, a quilt on her design wall, and lots of fabric—Bonnie's quilt dreams. That kindled a fire in me to bring her quilt dreams to life. My sister left me many things: her love, friendship, and a passion for quilting. As I worked on those quilts, I felt her guidance along the way. I conquered mitered corners, sashing, Y-seams, and appliqué. Bonnie was still teaching me. I imagined her chuckling gently as I ripped seams and somehow it eased the pain of missing her."

— *Diane Breitsprecker*

materials

QUILT SIZE
83" x 83"

BLOCK SIZE
9½" unfinished, 9" finished

QUILT TOP
1 package 10" print squares
2¼ yards of background fabric
   or 1 package of 10"
   background squares

BORDER
1½ yards

BINDING
¾ yard

BACKING
7¾ yards - vertical seam(s)
   or 2¾ yards 108" wide

SAMPLE QUILT
Artisan Batiks Solids - Prisma Dyes Lava Flow
by Lunn Studios for Robert Kaufman

1 cut

From the background fabric, cut:

- (4) 9½" strips across the width of the fabric. Subcut each strip into (4) 9½" squares for a **total of (16)** 9½" background squares. Set these aside for the moment.
- (4) 10" strips across the width of the fabric. Subcut each strip into (4) 10" squares for a **total of (16)** 10" background squares.

Note: If you are using precut 10" background squares, trim 16 squares to 9½" and set 10 squares aside for another project.

2 make half-square triangles

Set 10 print squares aside for another project.

Mark a line from corner to corner once on the diagonal on the reverse side of each 10" background square. **2A**

Place a marked background square atop a 10" print square with right sides facing. Sew on both sides of the marked line using a ¼" seam allowance. Cut on the marked line. Open each unit and press the seam toward the print fabric. Trim the units to 9½". Each pair of sewn squares will yield 2 half-square triangles. Repeat to **make 32** print/background half-square triangles. **2B**

Mark a line from corner to corner once on the diagonal on the reverse side of 8 print squares. Pair each marked print square with a contrasting print square. Repeat the previous instructions to **make 16** print/print half-square triangles. **2C**

Block Size: 9½" unfinished, 9" finished

3 arrange & sew

Select (4) 9½" background squares, 8 print/background half-square triangles, and 4 print/print half-square triangles. Arrange them in 4 rows as shown, paying special attention to the orientation of each block. Sew the blocks together in rows. Press the seam allowances of rows 1 and 3 to the left and rows 2 and 4 to the right. **3A**

Nest the seams and sew the rows together to complete 1 quadrant. **Make 4**. **3B**

2A

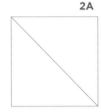

2B

2C

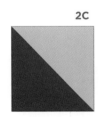

1 Mark a line from corner to corner once on the diagonal on the reverse side of each 10" background square and on (8) 10" print squares.

2 Place a marked background square atop an unmarked 10" print square with right sides facing. Sew on both sides of the marked line using a ¼" seam allowance. Cut on the marked line.

3 Open each unit and press the seam toward the darker fabric. Trim the units to 9½". Each pair of sewn squares will yield 2 half-square triangles. Repeat to make 32 print/background and 16 print/print half-square triangles.

4 Arrange (4) 9½" background squares, 8 print/ background, and 4 print/print half-square triangles as shown. Sew the units together in rows. Nest the seams and sew the rows together to complete 1 quadrant. Make 4.

3A
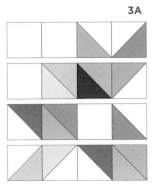

3B
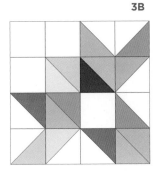

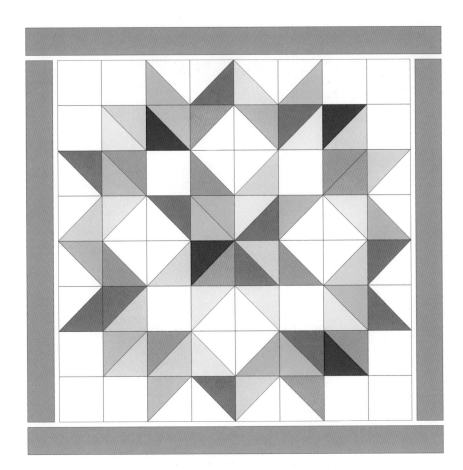

Referring to the diagram on the left, lay out the quadrants in **2 rows** of **2 quadrants** each, paying special attention to the orientation of each quadrant. Sew the quadrants together in rows. Press the seam allowance of the top row to the left and the bottom row to the right. Nest the seams and sew the rows together to complete the quilt center.

4 border

Cut (8) 6″ strips across the width of the fabric. Sew the strips together end-to-end to make 1 long strip. Trim the border from this strip.

Refer to Borders (pg. 110) in the Construction Basics to measure and cut the border. The strips are approximately 72½″ for the sides and approximately 83½″ for the top and bottom.

5 quilt & bind

Layer the quilt with batting and backing and quilt. After the quilting is complete, square up the quilt and trim away all excess batting and backing. Add binding to complete the quilt. See Construction Basics (pg. 110) for binding instructions.

For the tutorial and everything
you need to make this quilt visit:
www.msqc.co/Blockv7issue4

At Home Among the Trees
Aspen Quilt featuring Penny Layman

Penny Layman is a Colorado-based quilter with a flair for vintage modern style. She is a master of foundation paper piecing, and we are delighted to publish her beautiful Aspen quilt in Block Magazine. Read on to get to know a bit more about this talented designer:

Can you tell us a little bit about yourself and how you got into quilting?

"Out of necessity, my mom sewed a lot of my clothes when I was a child. She taught me how to sew by hemming tea towels. When I took Home Economics classes in middle school, my interest in sewing blossomed. I mostly sewed household items like pillows, cushions, curtains and ill-fitting clothing until I started quilting about twelve years ago."

"I had several friends who were quilters and I decided I wanted to learn about quilting, not to be a quilter, but just to see what they were so excited about. I set up times to watch each of them in their studios and before I knew it, I started quilting."

What inspired you to make this quilt? Why is it called "Aspen"?

"Living in Colorado, one of the most beautiful and striking seasons is fall. My husband and I love to hike and backpack and oftentimes we find ourselves hiking through aspen groves. I love the way the aspen leaves whisp in the wind. This quilt is inspired by those leaves and their color change in the fall."

What colors do you like to quilt with the most? What influences your color choices?

"My favorite color is green, but I find myself using blue hues a lot in my quilting. Bright happy colors are my go-tos. The colors I ultimately go for in a quilt depend on the feeling I want it to portray. Most of the time I choose colors that bring a smile and joy.

However, one of my most recent quilts was for a friend that had been diagnosed with pancreatic cancer. I chose colors for that quilt that were peaceful and quiet."

What techniques do you enjoy using the most when quilting? Do you have any tips or tricks for those who will make your quilt?

"I fell in love with paper piecing before I even knew what it was called or how to do it. It was kind of like the first time I tried cilantro. I didn't know what I was tasting but I knew I had to have more of it! Back then, there was little to no online information about paper piecing. I did find a few bloggers, so I asked them as many questions as I could and then taught myself."

As far as tips for making the Aspen quilt, here are a couple I wrote down as I was making it:

• If your velvet is not 100% cotton, use a pressing cloth when ironing.
• Use a seam roller before ironing seams.
• Use a leather mallet to hammer bulky seams before quilting.

What else would you like to add about your quilt?

"When I chose the quilting pattern for Aspen, I wanted a design that wouldn't detract from the piecing. I chose the alternating design of squares and circles to give the quilting almost a looking glass effect into the block design."

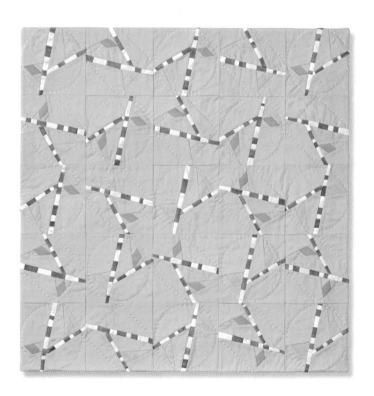

materials

QUILT SIZE
30" x 30"

BLOCK SIZE
6½" unfinished, 6" finished

QUILT TOP
2¼ yards aqua fabric
¼ yard bright yellow velvet
¼ yard dark yellow velvet
¼ yard tan velvet*
¼ yard cream velvet*

BINDING
½ yard

BACKING
1 yard

OTHER
Cardstock or index cards
Add-A-Quarter Ruler - optional

*Note: If using fabric less than 56" wide, you will need double
the amount of each fabric noted with an *.*

SAMPLE QUILT
Kona Cotton Solids by Robert Kaufman Fabrics

1 print

Make 25 copies of the block pattern found on page 85 or visit **msqc.co/aspenblock** to download the PDF. Be sure the document is printed at 100% scale and each block measures 6".

2 cut

From the aqua fabric:

- Cut (6) 5" strips across the width of the fabric.
  - Subcut each of 3 strips into (8) 5" squares. Label this stack A-5.
  - Subcut 1 of the strips into (1) 5" square and (14) 5" x 2½" rectangles. Add the 5" square to the A-5 stack. Subcut each of the 5" x 2½" rectangles once in half to yield 2½" squares. Label the stack of 2½" squares B-1/B-3.

- Subcut each of 2 strips into (13) 5" x 2¾" rectangles. Label this stack B-5. You will have 1 extra rectangle you can put aside for another project.

- Cut (5) 4½" strips across the width of the fabric.
  - Subcut each of 4 strips into (6) 4½" x 6½" rectangles. Label this stack B-7.
  - Subcut (1) 4½" x 6½" rectangle from the remaining strip. Add the rectangle to the B-7 stack.

- Cut (4) 3½" strips across the width of the fabric.
  - Subcut each of 2 strips into (13) 3½" x 3" rectangles. Label this stack A-4. You will have 1 extra rectangle you can put aside for another project.
  - Subcut each of the 2 remaining strips into (13) 3½" x 2½" rectangles. Label this stack B-4. You will have 1 extra rectangle you can put aside for another project.

- Cut (2) 2½" strips across the width of the fabric.
  - Subcut 1 of the strips into (16) 2½" squares. Add these to the 2½" squares labeled B-1/B-3.
  - Subcut (6) 2½" squares from the second strip and add these to the B-1/B-3 stack.

- Cut (2) 1½" strips across the width of the fabric.
  - Subcut each of the strips into (25) 1½" squares. Label this stack of squares as A-2/A-3.

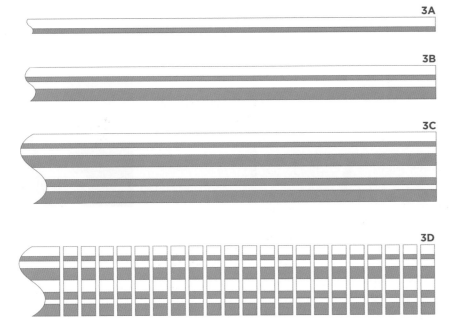

3A

3B

3C

3D

1 Place an A-1 square in position on the back side of the paper template. Pin in place.

2 Place a piece of cardstock along the line between A-1 and A-2. Fold the paper pattern back over the cardstock and then use a ruler and rotary cutter to trim the fabric ¼" away from the folded paper.

3 Align the bottom edge of an A-2 square on top of the A-1 square. Sew on the A-1/A-2 line.

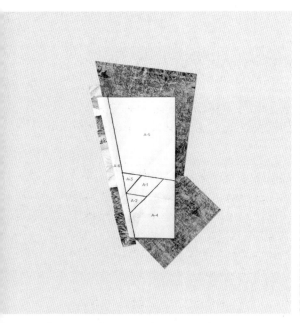

4 Repeat the previous steps and attach pieces A-3, A-4, A-5, and A-6 to the paper pattern.

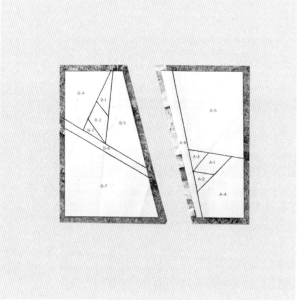

5 Follow the same steps to attach pieces B-1 through B-7 to the B portion of the paper pattern. Trim the fabric ¼" away from the outer edge of both portions of the block.

6 Remove the paper from the back of the block. Sew the 2 portions together to complete the block.

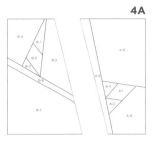

4A

4B

4C

4D

From the bright yellow and dark yellow fabrics:

- Cut (2) 2½" strips across the width of each fabric. Subcut 2½" squares from each strip. Label this stack of squares as A-1/B-2.

Note: You can decide how many A-1 and B-2 pieces you would like of the bright yellow or dark yellow fabric. Once you determine this, cut the appropriate number of 2½" squares from each color. You will need a **total of 50** A-1/B-2 squares.

From the tan and cream fabrics:

- Cut 4 strips across the width of each fabric. The widths of the strips should vary anywhere from 1" wide to 2" wide.*

*__Note__: If you are using fabric that is less than 56" in width, you'll need to cut 8 strips from both the tan and cream fabrics instead of 4.

3 strip piecing

Select 1 of the tan strips and 1 of the cream strips. Place the strips, right sides facing, and sew them together along 1 long edge. Press toward the darker fabric. Repeat with all remaining tan and cream strips. **3A**

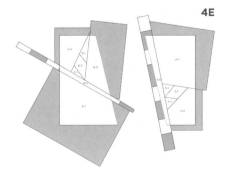

4E

Select 2 of the tan/cream paired strips. Place the paired strips, right sides facing. Be sure the cream of 1 paired strip is on top of the tan from the other set. Sew together along 1 long edge. Press toward the darker fabric to create a 4-strip set. **3B**

Place the 4-strip sets on top of each other with the right sides facing. Be sure the cream of 1 set is on top of the tan from the other set. Sew together along 1 long edge. Press toward the darker fabric to create a strip set. **3C**

Note: If you are using fabric less than 56" wide and cut 8 strips of each color instead of 4, repeat the previous steps to make a second strip set.

Cut the strip set(s) into (50) 1" segments. Label this stack of pieces as A-6/B-6. **3D**

4 paper piecing

Cut each of your block patterns into 2 pieces along the blue line. **4A**

Note: The stacks we labeled previously correspond to the pieces labeled on the block pattern.

On the reverse side of the pattern piece (the side that's blank), place an A-1 square in position. Pin the piece in place. The reverse side of the fabric should face the reverse side of the paper pattern. Pin the piece in place. **4B**

Turn the piece over and place a piece of cardstock on the line between piece A-1 and A-2. Fold the paper back over the cardstock. Use a ruler and rotary cutter to trim the fabric. After trimming, you will have a straight, ¼″ seam allowance showing beyond the edge of the fold. **4C**

Place an A-2 square on top of the A-1 piece, aligned with the trimmed edge and with right sides together. Pin in place to avoid having it slip. Turn the piece over and sew on the line that's marked between A-1 and A-2, extending the seam line past each end of the marked line by at least ¼″. Press piece 2 open using a dry iron. **4D**

Continue the process by placing the cardstock on the line between A-1 and A-3 and trim using your ruler and rotary cutter. Place an A-3 square on the trimmed line with right sides together and sew in place. Continue to sew and trim, adding each A piece in the numerical order given on the foundation pattern until the unit is complete. After the A portion is complete, repeat the steps to add the B-1 through B-7 pieces to the B portion of the block. **4E**

When you have completed an A piece and a B piece, trim ¼″ away from the outer edge of both pattern pieces. **4F**

Sew the A piece to the B piece. **Make 25** blocks. Remove the paper from the backside of each block. **4G**

Block Size: 6½″ unfinished, 6″ finished

5 arrange & sew

Use the diagram to the right to lay out the blocks in **5 rows** of **5 blocks**. Notice the orientation of the blocks in the

diagram. When you are pleased with your arrangement, sew the blocks together to form rows. Press the seams of the odd-numbered rows to the left and the seams of the even-numbered rows to the right. Sew the rows together and press to complete the quilt center.

6 quilt & bind

Layer the quilt with batting and backing and quilt. After the quilting is complete, square up the quilt and trim away all excess batting and backing. Add binding to complete the quilt. See Construction Basics (pg. 110) for binding instructions.

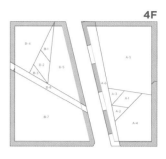

4F

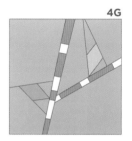

4G

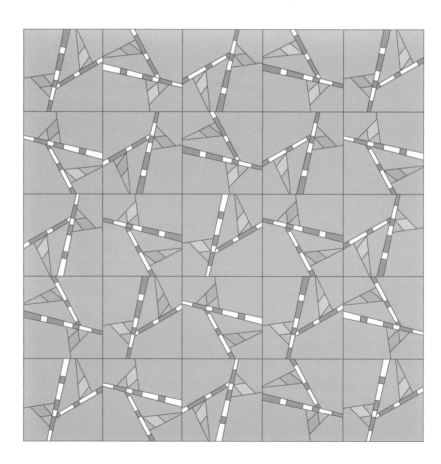

shown at 100%

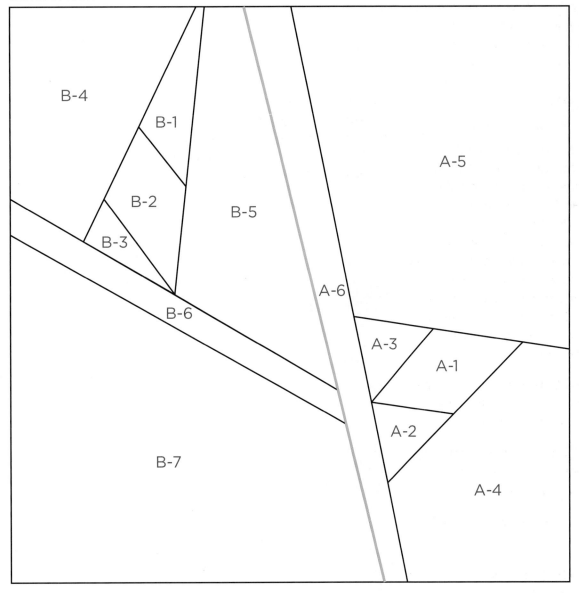

Bonus Project
Aspen Table Runner

PROJECT SIZE
29" x 8"

BLOCK SIZE
6½" unfinished, 6" finished

PROJECT TOP
½ yard dark gray fabric
¼ yard red fabric
¼ yard medium gray fabric
¼ yard light gray fabric
¼ yard white fabric

BINDING
¼ yard

BACKING
½ yard

OTHER
Cardstock or index cards
Add-A-Quarter Ruler - optional

SAMPLE QUILT
Cardinal Noel - Decorative Words by
Susan Winget for Wilmington Prints

1 cut

From the dark gray fabric:
- Cut (1) 5" strip across the width of the fabric. Subcut (4) 5" squares and (4) 5" x 2¾" rectangles. Label the stack of squares A-5. Label the stack of rectangles B-5.

- Cut (1) 4½" strip across the width of the fabric. Subcut (4) 4½" x 6½" rectangles. Label the stack of rectangles B-7. Trim the remainder of the strip to 1½". Subcut (8) 1½" squares from the strip. Label the stack of squares A-2/A-3.

- Cut (1) 3½" strip across the width of the fabric. Subcut (4) 3½" x 3" rectangles and (4) 3½" x 2½" rectangles from the strip. Label the stack of 3½" x 3" rectangles A-4. Label the stack of 3½" x 2½" rectangles B-4.

- Cut (1) 2 ½" strip across the width of the fabric. Subcut (8) 2½" squares from the strip. Label the stack of squares B-1/B-3.

From the red fabric:
- Cut (1) 2½" strip across the width of the fabric. Subcut (8) 2½" squares. Label this stack A-1/B-2.

From the light gray, medium gray, and white fabrics:
- Cut 4 strips across the width of each fabric. The widths of the strips should vary anywhere from 1" wide to 2" wide.

2 print & sew

Make 4 copies of the block pattern found on page 85 or visit **msqc.co/aspenblock** to download the PDF. Be sure the document is printed at 100% scale and each block measures 6".

Follow the method used on page 83 to create a strip set. Use all 12 of the strips you cut from the white, light gray, and medium gray fabrics. Sew each of the gray strips to a white strip. Sew a pair of sewn strips with the light gray strip to a pair of sewn strips with the medium gray strip. Be sure there is always a white strip separating the gray strips. Repeat to **make 3**.

Sew the 3 sets of sewn strips together to create a strip set that features 3 fabrics and is 12 strips wide. After completing it, cut (4) 1" segments, perpendicular to the seams, from the strip set. Set the rest of the strip set aside for the sashing and

border. Subcut each of the 1" segments to yield 2 segments that are at least 1" x 7" and 1" x 5". Use the 1" x 7" segment for piece A-6. Use the 1" x 5" segment for B-6.

Follow the instructions on page 83 to piece 4 blocks.

Block Size: 6½" unfinished, 6" finished

3 arrange & sew

From the remainder of the strip set you set aside earlier, cut 1½" segments perpendicular to the seams. Sew the segments together to form 1 long strip. From the long strip, cut (3) 1½" x 6½" sashing strips. Set the rest of the long strip aside for the border.

Lay out the **4 blocks** in a single row with a sashing strip placed between them. Reference the diagram below as

needed. When you're happy with your arrangement, sew the blocks and sashing strips together to form a row. Press the seams towards the blocks.

4 border

Pick up the remainder of the long strip you set aside earlier. Trim the borders from this strip.

Refer to Borders (pg. 110) in the Construction Basics to measure, cut, and attach the borders. The strips are approximately 27½" for the top and bottom and approximately 8½" for the sides.

Note: The borders on this project are sewn on to the top and bottom edges first and then the sides.

5 quilt & bind

Layer the project with batting and backing and quilt. After the quilting is complete, square up the project and trim away all excess batting and backing. Add binding to complete the table runner. See Construction Basics (pg. 110) for binding instructions.

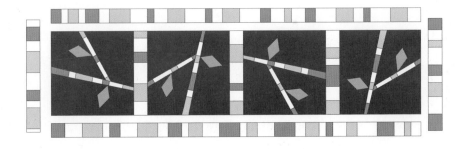

For the tutorial and everything you need to make this quilt visit:
www.msqc.co/Blockv7issue4

88

Love It Up
Dresden Blooms Quilt

"When I decide whether or not to add an interest, hobby, or relationship into my life, one of the main gates that decision has to pass through is, "Will this new thing enhance community and belonging in my life?" I used to think that I thought this way because I'm a passionate extrovert. Now I think I see through these eyes because belonging and community are some of the core things we all long for as humans.

"I took my first ever quilt class 33 years ago and I loved it. By the end of the course, I was in love and committed for life! In the early years of my quilt life, the fledgling quilt guild that met at Gettysburg's only quilt shop was my life line for inspiration, ideas, new tools and techniques. I loved having a community who was as excited about this newly opened world as I was.

"I've now been in North Carolina for nine years, have only been connected to a guild for three of those years and have a few fellow quilters in my life. But there are a couple of ways I bring community into my quilting life aside from being with other quilters.

"When I finish a quilt it's now my habit to bring it to my next community gathering and just let it be in the midst of the space for the time that we meet. I've brought it to my yoga class, my house dinner group, my book club. This is where being a passionate extrovert comes in handy. At the start, I show my newly born quilt and tell people whatever story is connected to it and explain that I've brought it so the group can 'love it up' before it goes to it's new home. By 'love it up' I mean they get to admire it, to send some loving energy along to the recipient and be a witness for this work I've done, mostly alone. Without exception, people have always loved being part of this and thanked me. So, if this resonates with you, give it a try! I bet you'll be glad you did!

"When I was first introduced to Hawaiian quilting, something I loved learning about was the tradition of the maker sleeping under the quilt before sending it to its new home. I love doing this. And in recent years, whenever we have an overnight guest and I have a finished quilt that hasn't yet left it's birth house, I offer our guest the opportunity to sleep under it. Part of my offer is telling about where the quilt is headed. Again, people feel they are part of a blessing of sorts when they get to do this. It's fun!

"In the end, I think quilting encourages community just because of what it is and how it gets made, whether that is gathering to quilt a wedding quilt that many have contributed blocks to or fabric shopping with an artist friend because he has such a good eye for color. However you connect the dots, quilting has so many doors that can be access points for community and belonging, for helping people heal and know they are loved. I hope it's in my life for the long haul, because it's in my heart to stay!"

— *Amanda Ann Godwin*

materials

QUILT SIZE
81½" x 81½"

BLOCK SIZE
24" unfinished, 23½" finished

QUILT TOP
1 roll 2½" print strips
2½ yards background fabric
2¼ yards of solid fabric
1½ yards of 3 different solid fabrics

BORDER
1½ yards

BINDING
¾ yard

BACKING
7½ yards - vertical seam(s)
    or 2½ yards 108" wide

OTHER
Missouri Star Large Dresden Plate for 10" Squares
½ yard Heat n Bond Lite

SAMPLE QUILT
Autumn Beauties by Studio RK for Robert Kaufman

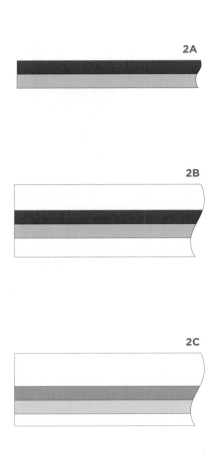

2A

2B

2C

3A

1 cut

From the background fabric, cut 6 strips each of the following widths: 5", 4", 3", and 2".

From the 2¼ yards of solid fabric, cut (3) 24" strips across the width of fabric. From each of the (3) 1½ yards of solid fabric, cut (2) 24" strips across the width of each fabric. Subcut (1) 24" square from each strip. You will need a **total of (9)** 24" squares of the 4 different solids. **Cut (9)** 5¼" solid squares which match each of your (9) 24" squares from the remaining pieces of fabric.

From the Heat n Bond Lite, cut (3) 5" strips across the width of the adhesive web. Subcut each strip into (3) 5" squares for a **total of 9**.

2 make strip sets

Select 24 print strips for your quilt and set the remaining strips aside for the bonus wall hanging or another project.

Lay 2 contrasting print strips right sides together. Sew the strips together along 1 long side using a ¼" seam allowance. **Make 12** strip sets. **2A**

Sew a 4" background strip to the top and a 3" background strip to the bottom of a strip set. Open and press the seam allowances in 1 direction. **Make 6**. **2B**

Sew a 5" background strip to the top and a 2" background strip to the bottom

of a strip set. Open and press the seam allowances in 1 direction. **Make 6**. **2C**

3 make blades

Lay a strip set right side up on your cutting surface. Align the wide edge of the Dresden template with the top of the strip set. Carefully trim along both sides of the template. Without disturbing the template, pull the strip set away and trim the extra fabric from the small end of the template. Rotate the template 180° and align the wide edge of the template along the bottom edge. **3A**

Trim along the edge of the template, move the strip set away, and trim the extra fabric. Continue in this manner to trim dresden blades from each strip set. **Note:** For more variation, align the small end of the template with the edges of the strip set before trimming some blades. Each strip set will yield at least 15 blades and a **total of 180** are needed. **Note:** If your strip sets are long enough for 16 blades from each, the extra blades can be set aside for the bonus project.

Note: You have the option to leave the tips of your blades straight. If you choose straight tips you can skip to section 4.

To create pointed blades, fold 1 blade in half lengthwise, right sides together. Sew across the wide end of the folded blade. **3B**

Trim the folded corner to reduce the bulk and turn right side out. Poke the corner

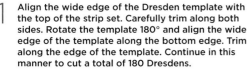

1 Align the wide edge of the Dresden template with the top of the strip set. Carefully trim along both sides. Rotate the template 180° and align the wide edge of the template along the bottom edge. Trim along the edge of the template. Continue in this manner to cut a total of 180 Dresdens.

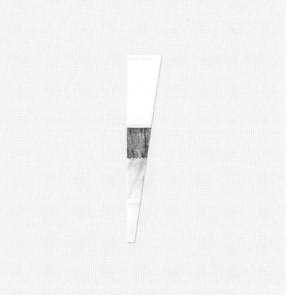

2 To create pointed blades, fold 1 blade in half lengthwise, right sides together. Sew across the wide end of the folded blade.

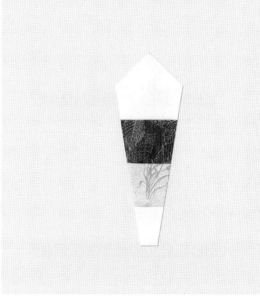

3 Trim the folded corner to reduce the bulk and turn right side out. Poke the corner out and press. Repeat the instructions to fold, sew, trim, turn, and press each blade.

4 Sew 5 blades together as shown to form a quadrant, being sure to alternate prints and placement of the pieced sections. Make 4 quadrants.

5 Sew the 4 quadrants together to complete a Dresden circle. Make 9 Dresden circles.

6 Fold (1) 24" square in half both ways and crease to mark the center. Lay 1 Dresden circle on top of the square and align the seams with the center creases. Pin as needed. Appliqué the circle in place around the outer edge using a blanket or zigzag stitch.

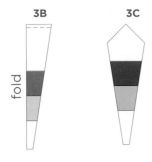

3B   3C

fold

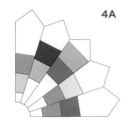

4A

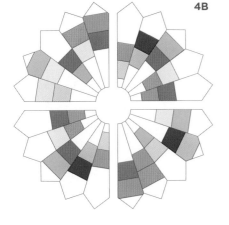

4B

out and press. Repeat the instructions to fold, sew, trim, turn, and press each blade. **Make 180**. **3C**

4 block construction

Sew 5 blades together as shown to form a quadrant, being sure to alternate prints and placement of the pieced sections. **Make 4** quadrants. **4A**

Sew the 4 quadrants together to complete a Dresden circle. **Make 9** Dresden circles. **4B**

Fold (1) 24" square in half both ways and crease to mark the center. Lay 1 Dresden circle on top of the square and align the seams with the center creases. Pin as needed. Using a blanket or zigzag stitch, appliqué the circle in place around the outer edge. **4C**

Using the template for the 5" circle on page 94, trace a circle onto the paper side of a 5" adhesive web square. Following the manufacturer's instructions, fuse the adhesive web square to the wrong side of a 5¼" solid square that matches your 24" square. Follow the traced line to cut the circle from the fused square. Remove the paper backing from the adhesive and throw it away.

Fold the fused circle in half both ways and crease to mark the center. Lay the fused circle atop the appliquéd Dresden circle, adhesive side down, and lining up the center creases with the seams of the Dresden. When you are happy with your placement, fuse the circle to the

Dresden according to the manufacturer's instructions. Using a blanket or zigzag stitch, appliqué the circle in place. Repeat the process to appliqué the remaining Dresdens and center circles to solid squares. **Make 9** blocks. **4D**

Block Size: 24" unfinished, 23½" finished

5 arrange & sew

Referring to the diagram on page 94, lay out your blocks in **3 rows** of **3 blocks** each. Sew the blocks together in rows. Press the seam allowances of the top and bottom rows to the left and the middle row to the right. Nest the seams and sew the rows together to complete the quilt center. Press the seams down.

6 border

Cut (8) 6" strips across the width of the border fabric. Sew the strips together end-to-end to make 1 long strip. Trim the border from this strip.

Refer to Borders (pg. 110) in the Construction Basics to measure, cut, and attach the borders. The strips are approximately 71" for the sides and approximately 82" for the top and bottom.

7 quilt & bind

Layer the quilt with batting and backing and quilt. After the quilting is complete, square up the quilt and trim away all excess batting and backing. Add binding to complete the quilt. See Construction Basics (pg. 110) for binding instructions.

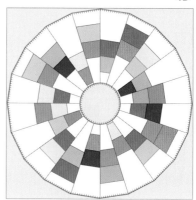

straight edge option

4C

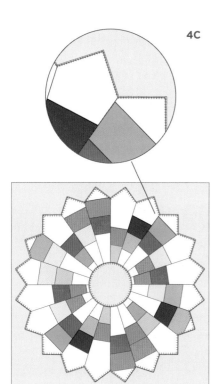

5" circle

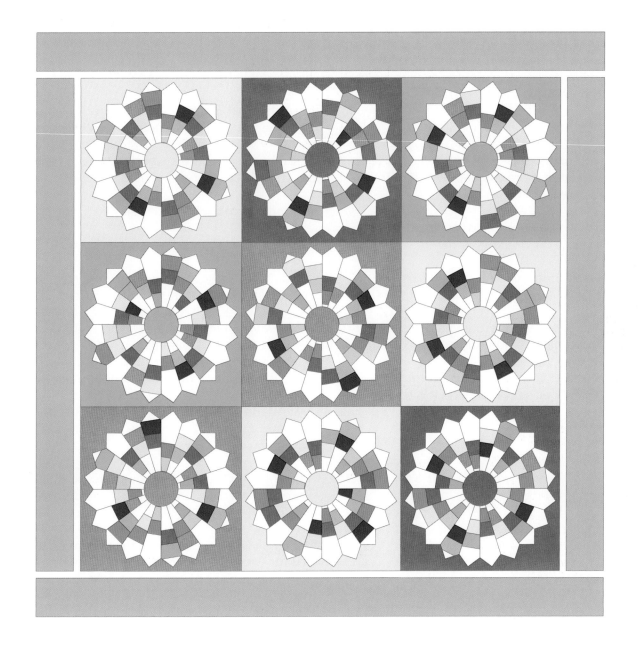

Jenny forced a knowing expression, maneuvering the conversation with care. "I was surprised, too. Did you ever get to see it?"

Loretta's scowl turned her lips into a full downward curve, her arms crossed over her chest. "Does it matter? She handed it off to someone who barely spent any time with her."

"Blair and her mother were very close."

"Not Blair, you ninny. You. Blair handed it off to you." Loretta's hard glare was a one-eighty from the tearful woman who'd invited her in.

"Oh, I'm sorry. I'd be happy to show it to you, but it's disappeared. You wouldn't know—"

"I would have helped her with it in a heartbeat. I would have done anything for Gina. And the same for Blair." Loretta towered over Jenny, her fists clenched, and Jenny wondered what kind of violence the woman would find acceptable.

"Lo?" Jenny stood and waited until Loretta's angry eyes lifted to look at her. "Blair's quilt is gone."

"You mean Gina's quilt?"

"Yes. Someone stole it, and we've already contacted the authorities." Jenny watched Loretta's face shuffle through emotions of anxiety, fear, and anger.

"You don't really think it was stolen, do you? What if you misplaced it?"

Jenny narrowed her eyes and dug a hand in her pocket. She pulled out the little button. "I think this might belong to you."

Loretta flushed a deep red and Jenny half expected her ears to start streaming again. Loretta reached over, snatching the button. "It does. Now, I think it's time you left."

"Loretta, did you take the quilt?"

"I did no such thing." Loretta's jaw tightened, and her hands shook ever so slightly.

"But the quilt is gone." Jenny's theory was crumbling, and she felt guilty for confronting the poor woman.

"I didn't take it. Sure, I wanted to help. I would have taken it if I could, but I couldn't find it."

"When did you talk to Claudia?"

"Yesterday morning. She let me in the studio."

"You mean Michelle? Claudia's daughter, Michelle, is my assistant. She was at the studio, not Claudia."

"I know who I mean. Claudia let me in. We were reminiscing about Gina. She used to be good friends with Gina when they were teens. Michelle wouldn't have been able to do that, now, would she?"

"No." Jenny felt the tide of questions shifting inside her and pulled out one more. "Where was the quilt when you were there?"

"You had it. Claudia said you took the quilt home." Loretta glared at Jenny. "Blair should have come to me."

Jenny excused herself. Claudia had been there in her studio. She thought of the broken necklace Officer Wilkins had found under the worktable. Michelle had claimed it was her mother's, which meant Claudia had been in the studio alone. Claudia was the missing piece. But why would she want to steal Gina's quilt?

***

Ron had met Jenny at the studio on his way home from the Peters' house and was now retrieving a spool of gray thread for her while she waited in the car. She watched as the light came on and Ron's silhouette appeared in the window. A door slammed in the alley behind her and a shiver ran down her spine.

She gripped her purse and looked out the car window. The sound had come from the direction of Sam's food truck. Jenny knew she should stay where she was, but she couldn't just stand idly by if someone was causing trouble for the Peters family again. She got out of the car to see what was happening.

A light flipped on in the food truck. The urge to go and help coursed through her. She didn't need to be a hero, but a witness could make all the difference if the Peters were getting robbed again. Jenny moved around the vehicle to get a better look and dialed Ron. She watched for his silhouette to answer his phone, but he didn't. The voicemail hit, and she took a deep breath.

"Ron, answer your phone! I'm headed to Sam's food truck. Call the police and come quick!"

She hung up and dialed again as a figure moved across the alley behind the food truck.

It could be nothing, she told herself, and hung up the unanswered phone. She moved across the grass as quickly as she could. Still feeling the pain that lingered in her shoulder, she flattened herself against the side of the trailer. Inside, she could hear someone rummaging slowly through the truck, like they had all the time in the world.

Jenny dug into her purse until her fingers wrapped around a metal shaft. She pulled it out to find the screwdriver she'd put in there the day before after Ron fixed the doorknob. The metal handle was cold in her grip, and she moved carefully around the vehicle. The sounds inside the truck stilled completely, and the light flipped off.

The back door handle jiggled, and Jenny set her shoulder against the door as someone pushed back. She jammed the screwdriver through the handle and into the locking mechanism, holding the door in place.

The culprit slammed against the door. Jenny leaned on it from the outside as Ron appeared almost at the same time as sirens blared from down the street. "Jenny!" he called, putting a hand against the door as whoever was in there banged harder. Then it stopped.

The pause was disconcerting. Shortly after, they heard movement at the other side of the truck. "Stay here," Ron whispered and followed the sound to the shuttered window.

Police officers called out behind her, and a masked figure ran out from a break in the alley. Jenny covered her mouth to keep from screaming. She watched Ron step forward as the metal awning lifted and a leg swung out of the window.

A young woman tumbled down from the window with a thump. A swath of strawberry blond hair fell from under the loose beanie she wore, and she cried out as Ron lifted her to her feet with a firm grip, maintaining his grasp to keep her from running away. Officer Wilkins and Dunn pounded down the alley toward them. Wilkins halted long enough to yell, "Freeze!" and aim his gun.

The girl obeyed, going completely still in Ron's arms, allowing Jenny to get a good look at her.

"Blair?"

to be continued...

Pop Stars

QUILT SIZE
67" x 75½"

BLOCK SIZE
9" unfinished, 8½" finished

QUILT TOP
1 package 10" print squares
½ yard accent fabric
1¾ yards background fabric
  - includes inner border

OUTER BORDER
1¼ yards

BINDING
¾ yard

BACKING
4¾ yards - vertical seam(s)
  or 2½ yards of 108" wide

SAMPLE QUILT
The Christmas Card by Sweetwater
for Moda Fabrics

QUILTING PATTERN
Pine Tree Meander

PATTERN
P. 14

Every Which Way But Goose

QUILT SIZE
76" x 84"

BLOCK SIZE
8½" x 16½" unfinished,
8" x 16" finished

QUILT TOP
4 packages 5" print squares
4 packages 5" background squares
½ yard coordinating print fabric
1 yard background fabric
  - includes border

BINDING
¾ yard

BACKING
5¼ yards – vertical seam(s)
  or 2½ yards 108" wide

SAMPLE QUILT
Wilmington Essentials - Bubble Up
by Hello Angel for Wilmington Prints

QUILT PATTERN
Feather Meandering

PATTERN
P. 22

Quilt As You Go Holiday Hexies Advent Calendar

PROJECT SIZE
36" x 42½"

BLOCK SIZE
2½" finished hexagon

PROJECT SUPPLIES
3 packages 5" print squares
Twin size batting
  (approximately 72" x 93")
1¾ yards accent fabric
1 yard green fabric

OTHER
Quilt As You Go 2½" Hexagon Set
  designed by Daisy & Grace for
  Missouri Star Quilt Company

SAMPLE PROJECT
Christmas Traditions by Dani
Mogstad for Riley Blake

PATTERN
P. 28

Ruby Sensation Sew-along Diamond Pinwheel Block

BLOCK SIZE
12½" unfinished, 12" finished

DIAMOND PINWHEEL BLOCK
½ yard fabric A or (6) 2½" strips

½ yard fabric B or (6) 2½" strips
½ yard fabric D or (6) 2½" strips
1 yard background fabric

Note: Fabric C is not used in the block for Part Three.

PATTERN
P. 34

Diamond Terrace

QUILT SIZE
90" x 95"

BLOCK SIZE
8 x 10½" unfinished, 7½" x 10"
finished

QUILT TOP
1 roll 2½" print strips
4 yards background fabric
  - includes inner border

OUTER BORDER
1¾ yards

BINDING
¾ yard

BACKING
8½ yards - vertical seam(s)
  or 3 yards of 108" wide

SAMPLE QUILT
Bloomington by Lella Boutique
for Moda Fabrics

QUILTING PATTERN
Paisley Feather

PATTERN
P. 44

Trick or Treat Street Table Runner

PROJECT SIZE
40" x 30"

BLOCK SIZE
10½" unfinished, 10" finished

PROJECT TOP
1 package 5" print squares
½ yard yellow solid fabric
  - includes inner border
¾ yard gray background fabric

BORDER
¾ yard

BINDING
½ yard

BACKING
1 yard

OTHER
Missouri Star Large Dresden Plate
  Template for 10" squares
¾ yard fusible web

SAMPLE QUILT
Ghosts and Ghouls by Stacy Iest Hsu
for Moda Fabrics

QUILTING PATTERN
Meander

PATTERN
P. 50

Mini Double Nine-Patch Quilt

QUILT SIZE
69" x 75¾"

BLOCK SIZE
7¼" unfinished, 6¾" finished

QUILT TOP
1 roll 2½" print strips
1 roll 2½" background strips
  - includes inner border
1¾ yards background fabric

OUTER BORDER
1¼ yards

BINDING
¾ yard

BACKING
4¾ yards - vertical seam(s)
  or 2½ yards of 108" wide

SAMPLE QUILT
October Morning by Kim Diehl for
Henry Glass

QUILTING PATTERN
Cotton Candy

PATTERN
P. 66

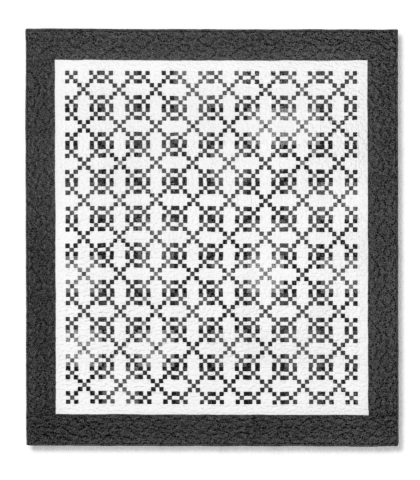

Jenny's Easy Carpenter's Star Quilt

QUILT SIZE
83" x 83"

BLOCK SIZE
9½" unfinished, 9" finished

QUILT TOP
1 package 10" print squares
2¼ yards of background fabric
    or 1 package of 10" background squares

BORDER
1½ yards

BINDING
¾ yard

BACKING
7¾ yards - vertical seam(s)
    or 2¾ yards 108" wide

SAMPLE QUILT
Artisan Batiks Solids - Prisma Dyes Lava Flow by Lunn Studios for Robert Kaufman

QUILTING PATTERN
Aztec Quilting

PATTERN
P. 72

Aspen Quilt

QUILT SIZE
30" x 30"

BLOCK SIZE
6½" unfinished, 6" finished

QUILT TOP
2¼ yards aqua fabric
¼ yard bright yellow velvet
¼ yard dark yellow velvet
¼ yard tan velvet*
¼ yard cream velvet*

BINDING
½ yard

BACKING
1 yard

OTHER
Cardstock or index card
Add-A-Quarter Ruler - optional

*Note: If using fabric less than 56" wide, you will need double the amount of each fabric noted with an *.*

SAMPLE QUILT
Kona Cotton Solids by Robert Kaufman Fabrics

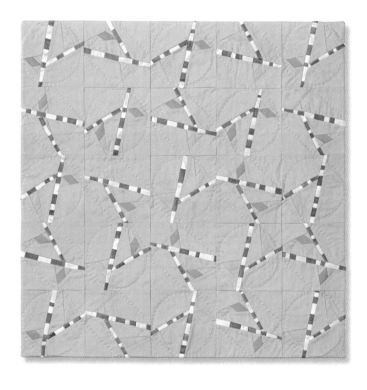

Aspen Table Runner

PROJECT SIZE
29" x 8"

BLOCK SIZE
6½" unfinished, 6" finished

PROJECT TOP
½ yard dark gray fabric
¼ yard red fabric
¼ yard medium gray fabric
¼ yard light gray fabric
¼ yard white fabric

BINDING
¼ yard

BACKING
½ yard

OTHER
Cardstock or index card
Add-A-Quarter Ruler - optional

PATTERN
P. 78

Dresden Blooms

QUILT SIZE
81½" x 81½"

BLOCK SIZE
24" unfinished, 23½" finished

QUILT TOP
1 roll 2½" print strips
2½ yards background fabric
2¼ yards of solid fabric
1½ yards of 3 different solid fabrics

BORDER
1½ yards

BINDING
¾ yard

BACKING
7½ yards - vertical seam(s)
    or 2½ yards 108" wide

OTHER
Missouri Star Large Dresden
    Plate for 10" Squares
½ yard Heat n Bond Lite

SAMPLE QUILT
Autumn Beauties by Studio RK for
Robert Kaufman

QUILTING PATTERN
Botanical Blossoms

PATTERN
P. 88

Construction Basics

General Quilting

- All seams are ¼" inch unless directions specify differently.
- Cutting instructions are given at the point when cutting is required.
- Precuts are not prewashed, therefore do not prewash other fabrics in the project.
- All strips are cut width of fabric.
- Remove all selvages.

Press Seams

- Use a steam iron on the cotton setting.
- Press the seam just as it was sewn right sides together. This "sets" the seam.
- With dark fabric on top, lift the dark fabric and press back.
- The seam allowance is pressed toward the dark side. Some patterns may direct otherwise for certain situations.
- Follow pressing arrows in the diagrams when indicated.
- Press toward borders. Pieced borders may demand otherwise.
- Press diagonal seams open on binding to reduce bulk.

Borders

- Always measure the quilt top 3 times before cutting borders.
- Start measuring about 4" in from each side and through the center vertically.
- Take the average of those 3 measurements.
- Cut 2 border strips to that size. Piece strips together if needed.
- Attach 1 to either side of the quilt.

- Position the border fabric on top as you sew. The feed dogs can act like rufflers. Having the border on top will prevent waviness and keep the quilt straight.
- Repeat this process for the top and bottom borders, measuring the width 3 times.
- Include the newly attached side borders in your measurements.
- Press toward the borders.

Binding

find a video tutorial at: www.msqc.co/006

- Use 2½" strips for binding.
- Sew strips end-to-end into 1 long strip with diagonal seams, aka the plus sign method (next). Press seams open.
- Fold in half lengthwise wrong sides together and press.
- The entire length should equal the outside dimension of the quilt plus 15" - 20."

Plus Sign Method

- Lay 1 strip across the other as if to make a plus sign right sides together.
- Sew from top inside to bottom outside corners crossing the intersections of fabric as you sew.
  Trim excess to ¼" seam allowance.
- Press seam open.

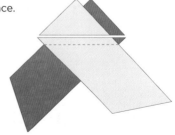

find a video tutorial at: www.msqc.co/001

Attach Binding

- Match raw edges of folded binding to the quilt top edge.
- Leave a 10" tail at the beginning.
- Use a ¼" seam allowance.
- Start in the middle of a long straight side.

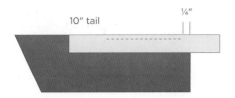

Miter Corners

- Stop sewing ¼" before the corner.
- Move the quilt out from under the presser foot.
- Clip the threads.
- Flip the binding up at a 90° angle to the edge just sewn.
- Fold the binding down along the next side to be sewn, aligning raw edges.
- The fold will lie along the edge just completed.
- Begin sewing on the fold.

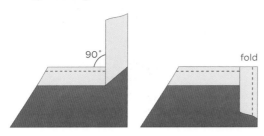

Close Binding

MSQC recommends The Binding Tool from TQM Products to finish binding perfectly every time.

- Stop sewing when you have 12" left to reach the start.
- Where the binding tails come together, trim excess leaving only 2½" of overlap.
- It helps to pin or clip the quilt together at the 2 points where the binding starts and stops. This takes the pressure off of the binding tails while you work.
- Use the plus sign method to sew the 2 binding ends together, except this time when making the plus sign, match the edges. Using a pencil, mark your sewing line because you won't be able to see where the corners intersect. Sew across.

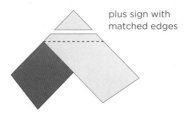

- Trim off excess; press seam open.
- Fold in half wrong sides together, and align all raw edges to the quilt top.
- Sew this last binding section to the quilt. Press.
- Turn the folded edge of the binding around to the back of the quilt and tack into place with an invisible stitch or machine stitch if you wish.